This Book belongs
To George Gewehr
1 - 31 - 01

D1604433

ANGELS TWENTY

Other Aviation Titles Published by McGraw-Hill

Aviation Week & Space Technology Military Pilot Reports
Aviation Week Group

The Blonde Knight of Germany
Raymond F. Toliver and Trevor J. Constable

Half a Wing, Three Engines and a Prayer: B-17s over Germany
Brian D. O'Neill

Messerschmidt ACES
Walter A. Musciano

The Martin B-26 Marauder
J. K. Havener

The C-130 Hercules: Tactical Airlift Missions 1956–1975
Sam McGowan

Once a Fighter Pilot
Jerry W. Cook

Unheeded Warning
Stephen A. Fredrick

American Aviation, An Illustrated History
Leroy Cook

Mach I and Beyond
Larry Reithmaler

U.S. Civil Aircraft Series, Volumes 1–9
Joseph P. Juptner

ANGELS TWENTY

A YOUNG AMERICAN FLYER
A LONG WAY FROM HOME

EDWARDS PARK

McGraw-Hill
New York   San Francisco   Washington, D.C.   Auckland   Bogotá
Caracas   Lisbon   London   Madrid   Mexico City   Milan
Montreal   New Delhi   San Juan   Singapore
Sydney   Tokyo   Toronto

Library of Congress Cataloging-in-Publication Data

Park, Edwards.
    Angels twenty : a young American flyer a long way from
home / Edwards Park. — [Updated ed.]
      p.   cm.
   ISBN 0-07-582125-7
   1. Park, Edwards. 2. World War, 1939–1945—
Campaigns—New Guinea. 3. World War, 1939–1945—Aerial
operations, American. 4. World War, 1939–1945—Personal
narratives, American. 5. United States. Air Force. Air Force.
Air Force, 5th—History. 6. Air pilots, Military—United
States—Biography. I. Title.
  D790.P358 1997
  940.54'26—dc20   96-44279
                                           CIP

McGraw-Hill

*A Division of The **McGraw·Hill** Companies*

1 2 3 4 5 6 7 8 9 0 BKP/BKP 9 0 1 0 9 8 7

ISBN 0-07-582125-7

*The sponsoring editor for this book was Shelley Chevalier, the editing
supervisor was Scott Amerman, and the production supervisor was
Suzanne Rapcavage. It was set in Fairfield by Don Feldman of
McGraw-Hill's Professional Book Group composition unit.*

Printed and bound by Quebecor Book Press.

CONTENTS

FOREWORD

This memoir was originally written for and published by the University of Queensland Press (Australia) in 1994. I'm grateful to them for encouraging my American publication.

Since this is a tale of long-ago events, I claim immunity to the need for exact truth. Certainly all the episodes described herein actually occurred. But I can't swear that their order of occurrence is deadly accurate. My log book is remarkably uncommunicative on that point, and I certainly don't trust my memory.

I have changed the names of the Beavers because I don't want the surviving members to jump all over me with claims that they didn't do what I said when I said they did, or that I misquoted them entirely. Actually, their memories are no better than mine.

Some of the early episodes are retold from *Nanette*, the book I wrote about my own assigned plane. Some later material, adapted for magazine use, appeared in *Smithsonian* and *Air & Space/Smithsonian*.

Edwards Park

PROLOGUE

My carburetor failed at 15,000 feet. I called the squadron leader and told him I couldn't keep up, that I'd have to stooge around over the mountains at this altitude while the rest of the Beavers continued their climb. Fighter sector had told us to look for unidentified planes at "Angels Twenty," which meant 20,000 feet, and the squadron had to get up there, even though the "bogies" were almost certainly one of the thunderclouds that boiled over the Owen Stanleys every afternoon.

"Okay Red Three," said the squadron leader. "We'll pick you up on the way home."

I circled lazily, alone, for once, in the little P-39 Airacobra that had been assigned to me. A mighty shoulder of cloud, bulging with white muscles, hunched upward over the great jagged peaks that formed the spine of New Guinea. I watched the writhing monster of mist swallow the lowering sun, and as shadow painted the rain forest far below, a lingering handful of rays fanned upward through gaps in the clouds, the way they often do in the tropical Pacific. No wonder the enemy had chosen that blazing sunburst as its battle flag.

Far above, the planes of my squadron gleamed in the last sunlight as they swung across the sky—the four distinct flights, Red, Blue, White, and Yellow, in patrol formation, four planes in each flight except my own Red Flight with only three.

I watched them orbit, then heard the sector call, "Beaver from Maple, all clear."

The squadron leader acknowledged, "Roger, Maple," and the little shapes, high against the sky, all rolled on their sides to lose altitude in a tight spiral. Their radar target was just a cloud; the day's work was done; we could head for the barn at last.

I began a wide turn to rejoin my friends, reluctant to end this precious interlude of free, undisciplined flight, yet oddly happy to return "home."

Then an urgent voice shocked me: "Beaver from Blue Four, eight o'clock low!"

And another: "Beaver, bogy at nine o'clock low!"

And I saw the planes draw tighter together and ease their spiral, noses down to gain speed.

I squirmed in my seat to scan the air below in the area that had been the squadron's "nine o'clock—directly abeam of them on their left. It didn't take me long to realize what they had seen. *I* was their target!

As they turned inexorably toward me, I hit my mike button and frantically called: "Beaver, Beaver! This is Red Three. You've got *me!*" And I stood my plane on its wing so they could see the American marking, the blue rondel with its white star.

For one breathtaking moment I faced my own squadron's attack—fifteen sleek little fighters swinging their sharp, yellow-tipped noses directly at me. I stared at the muzzles of fifteen nose cannon all leveled at me. I knew that thirty heavy machine guns, synchronized to fire through the propeller, were also aimed at me, plus sixty .30-caliber wing guns. I was the only target of 105 extremely lethal weapons. I held my breath, expecting to see a ripple of flame from all those muzzles and to sense the blinding thunder of exploding in midair.

Then the squadron leader's calm voice came into my earphones: "Don't shoot, boys. It's only Park."

I often recall that moment in 1943. That was how my old squadron would have looked to a Japanese pilot, unfortunate enough to have been caught alone that evening, over the mountains west of New Guinea's Ramu Valley, as the rays of that cloud-sheathed sun imitated his flag. To him, I suppose it would have been even more frightening than it was to me. He would have *known* that they'd shoot.

He wouldn't have known the truth about that fierce-looking squadron on the attack: that the pilots behind those glinting windscreens were little more than teenagers, bone-weary, hungry, wracked by persistent diarrhea, often trembling with strange fevers, and all too aware that their aircraft—plane for plane—couldn't match his.

We army flyers had been assigned to this theater of war because someone had to help hold the line here with outdated equipment while the best planes went to Europe to fight Hitler. The Pacific, according to grand strategy, was the domain of the U.S. Navy. Marines were supposed to handle island warfare along with army troops from Australia and New Zealand.

But New Guinea defied strategy. The planners found it bewilderingly big—after all, it's the world's second largest island after Greenland—and to winkle the entrenched Japanese out of it required some high-class ground troops—crack divisions of the Australian Imperial Force and, as they finally became trained, some American outfits. They needed lots of air support, more than the hard-pressed Royal Australian Air Force could hope to provide.

That's where the U.S. Fifth Air Force came in. It was formed of groups and squadrons originally destined for the Philippines, then rerouted to Australia and brought to combat readiness.

At first, Allied bombers got little fighter protection. The RAAF's P-40s (Kittyhawks) flung themselves at endless enemy raids on Port Moresby, spending themselves bravely against the Japanese Zeroes until a few American fighters arrived to help, among them our P-39s.

Those Airacobras were already obsolete. Britain had quickly rejected the export version—designated the P-400—as unusable in combat, but they served in New Guinea simply because they had to. I flew P-400s lots of times. They were terrible.

Once they reached the combat zone and went into action, the squadrons and groups of the Fifth Air Force were gladly forgotten by the Big Brass in Washington. Now the U.S. Army with its air forces could get down to business in Europe. New Guinea? All in good time. So new planes did not reach us— they went to England, instead. Adequate food did not reach us except when we could pull off some deals with the navy. Our rotation was painfully slow; many old pilots were still flying missions long after they should have been grounded.

My squadron was one of the forsaken units. All through 1943 we were pretty much left alone to operate as best we could in our little backwater of war. But thinking back on it as we do when we occasionally meet for a reunion—some two dozen elderly gentlemen, all rather short, all wearing spectacles and cursing the loss of what once was hawklike vision— we don't easily recall the bad times. We have to strain our memories to picture the fiery crashes of planes that simply fell apart from age and fatigue. We too often forget the names of the good companions who never returned from our swirling "soirees" over the mountains.

What we remember is the taste of quinine, almost as bad as the food, the stench of primitive latrines, the bugs in the sleeping bags, the whirring watchman's rattle that roused the early flight, the pump of adrenalin before takeoff, the tremble of knees after landing. We wince at the recollection of our jungle juice—the Doc's alcohol cut by Red Cross fruit drops melted in Lister-bag water, heavy with chemicals. And we sometimes sing as we did then:

> It's hardships, you bastards.
> You don't know what hardships are!

We realize—without condescension—that we were very different from today's young people. We were bigoted to a degree that is now painful to recall, chortling over racist jokes, treating our handful of squadron Jews with the wary courtesy reserved for foreign allies, and considering all women primarily sex objects.

We instinctively liked the Australians we met and worked beside, and were a little hurt when sometimes faced with their complaints about us—too many orchids bought for too many girls, too much steak ordered at too many expensive restaurants, in short, too bloody much money.

We went into action with what would now be considered unhealthy emotional inhibitions. For we accepted our defeats and losses in thin-lipped silence and our triumphs with the hangdog "Aw, shucks" bashfulness as much in fashion in the 1940s as the exuberant, hand-slapping "high-five" is today. We shared patriotism unblemished by cynicism, and a sense of humor that spared no sacred cow.

We did nothing very heroic or spectacular in New Guinea, but we tried to fulfill our obligations, and we had our moments. During those long, long years of war our futures changed drastically. For we grew up together, we band of Beavers. Our squadron may have been forsaken, but it was home, and it shaped us. And we can never forget it.

ANGELS TWENTY

"TOWNSVILLE? NEVER HEARD OF IT"

My first glimpse of Australia was a hazy, pale-blue smear on the horizon, coming and going through gusts of warm, misty rain. I remember how we all crowded onto the deck of our transport, disregarding the wet, watching the smudge of land gradually grow and take shape.

"Townsville?" Steve said. "Never heard of it."

"The second mate told me it's way up north. He says it's a staging area for New Guinea." Guppy put a hand on my shoulder. "Doesn't the thought of New Guinea make you feel great, Park?"

The three of us hung together at the starboard rail, the way we'd tended to adhere since we met in flying school. We'd been at sea three weeks from Hawaii, four weeks from San Francisco, which we'd left heading northward. Our Norwegian skipper may or may not have confused the Japanese spies, which, we were told, lurked behind every boulder on the California coast, but he'd certainly bewildered the hell out of us. "Are you sure we're getting off here?" I asked. "Maybe it's another trick."

"The second mate says it's the end of the line."

We fell silent, all thinking back over our strange, sometimes-but-not-always horrible voyage. With 297 other fighter pilots, we comprised the entire cargo of this small converted Norwegian freighter. We'd been crammed into a hold with five tiers of bunks. The adjoining latrine, much in use during the first days of the voyage, had a faulty drainage system that failed in a gale a few days out of Honolulu. Most of the time it sloshed with waste.

We ate—or tried to eat—twice a day, lining up with tin plates in another section of the hold. Every meal was exactly the same: two frankfurters, a slab of stale bread, and a piece of fruit. The frankfurters gradually turned green with mold, the bread ran out, and the fruit rotted. And the stench of the mess hall, mingling with that of the latrine, permeated the vessel from amidships aft.

Up forward, things were different. The cabin area was off limits to us, but we guessed it didn't stink. For here dwelt officers of the United States Army, from the rank of colonel down to second lieutenant. They had cabins to sleep in, bathrooms, a dining room with good food. They wore khaki pants and tailored shirts kept clean and pressed.

Oddly enough, we, too, were officers of the United States Army, almost all second lieutenants. But we carried the stigma of two small words: "Air Corps." That designation made us different, not really members of the officer corps, untutored in traditional military courtesies. None of us had gone to West Point, had ever left a calling card on the mahogany hall table of a base commander. None of us even owned a Sam Browne belt! Our khaki pants were stained and baggy. Our shirts (when we bothered to wear them) sagged with the weight of silver wings. We had never commanded men. The only thing each of us could do was fly a small airplane armed with machine guns. Obviously we had to be segregated from real officers.

Though the situation afforded us the pleasure of a good, solid gripe, we really didn't much care. The 300 of us talked our own language, enjoyed our own company. Being flyers, we quickly coped with seasickness. Being quick and resourceful— every American pilot had to have some college education back in 1942—we soon discovered ways to cadge a little food from the ground officers.

Some of us were formidable poker players and managed to wangle a profitable invitation "upstairs." Then there was always bribery. We had flight pay in our pockets, and the army cooks, the navy gun crews who manned our five-inchers, and the Norwegian swabbies who ran the ship could all be persuaded, by a buck or two, to slip us something to eat.

Life was easy—if rather dirty. We exercised twice a day, then lay in the sun on various patches of deck, reading, playing cards, arguing amiably, dozing, staring at the cobalt Pacific, hoping for a whale to spout. Boat drills broke the monotony. We learned Norwegian words from the sailors, watched the gun crews drill and the navy escort vessels swing across our bow and through our wake, weaving their security blanket.

In a tenuous way, we maintained contact with the world and its hurtling events. News bulletins, fresh from the wireless room, boomed at us through the ship's intercom system. Guadalcanal was turning into a blood bath. When we realized we were headed for the Southwest Pacific and not Alaska (we'd drawn Arctic clothing before leaving San Francisco to fool those ubiquitous Japanese spies), we began to pay considerable attention to the campaigns there and in New Guinea.

We were entertained on many evenings by the recollections of the first mate—his name was Bjorn something-or-other—of how he escaped the Nazi invasion of Norway. It was the same talk every time, coming over the speakers in our miserable bunkroom, and it always ended the same way: "Vell, anyvay, ve put on our shkees und ve shkeed over the Svedish border." To this day, if I hear an old veteran say, "Vell, anyvay," I fall upon him with glad cries.

On other evenings, we were briefed by our supernumerary passenger, a member of Chennault's American Volunteer Group, the "Flying Tigers," who was on his way back to the China-Burma area to rejoin his squadron of P-40s. He was a red-haired captain, tough, tense, yet wonderfully patient with us greenhorns as we listened anxiously to his talks and then swamped him with questions.

"Never, never try to turn with the Japanese," he told us again and again. "You've all been told that American planes are the envy of the world. Well, they're not. If you try to follow a Zero in a steep climb, you'll stall and spin, and he'll nail you. If you try to get away by turning, he'll turn inside you like a flash for a deflection shot, and that'll be it. Meet him head on, shoot, then ease up in a straight, shallow climb, keeping plenty of speed, and maybe you can turn back for another pass. If he gets on your tail, bang your stick forward and dive straight down. The Zero's not stressed to do that."

"Are we stressed to do that?" someone once asked.

"I don't know," he answered with a faint smile. "But I haven't lost the wings yet."

"Have you got any Japs?"

"Four."

"Do you like the P-40?"

"You bet. But we've got better stuff coming."

"How about the P-39?"

Steve, Guppy, and I pricked up our ears. We'd been flying the little P-39, the Bell Airacobra, in a training unit in Florida. We'd found it a dicey, difficult plane. Guppy'd rolled one into a ball on landing, and I'd managed to tumble in one—falling head over heels for a few turns until it straightened itself out. It would do that once in while, for its engine was mounted behind the cockpit to make room for a 37-millimeter cannon, and when the ammunition drum was empty, the center of gravity moved aft.

The Flying Tiger looked a little uneasy. "The 'Thirty-nine's OK if you know how to fly it. A lot of people don't, including me. It should be great for low-level work, but it hasn't got any altitude. Anyway, new planes are coming."

"Cold comfort," muttered Steve in my ear.

Well, the voyage was ending at last, one way or another, and now the three of us gazed with various attitudes at the gleaming tin roofs of Townsville, plainly in sight.

We'd recently been issued a small booklet about Australia, with a brief character sketch of the people, as though they were a homogeneous species like rhesus monkeys: They're friendly creatures who really mean it if, soon after meeting you, they ask you home for tea—which means dinner. Even nice people go to race tracks and bet on horses that run the wrong way. Their accent's odd ("Was I brought here to die?" asks the badly wounded American pilot, regaining consciousness in a hospital. "No, yesterdye," answers the Australian nurse), and they use words like "dinkum" and "cobber" and shout "coo-ee" at each other. If an Australian girl tells you she's "knocked up," it doesn't mean she's pregnant—just tired. That was about it.

I tried to remember everything I'd ever heard about this country. Down under. Kangaroos. The duck-billed platypus. Great wealth. I got that from a comic strip in boyhood days about "The Gumps," Andy Gump, his wife Min, and their son Chester. They were visited by Uncle Bim, from Australia, who was very rich and gave Chester a little airplane he could fly himself. It was a low-winged monoplane with an open cockpit, and Chester sat there with his head in the wind and flew around. That's what I wanted when I was a kid, and now I was about to set foot in Uncle Bim's country and fly a low-winged monoplane....

We now could see palm trees along an esplanade, a schooner moored at a pier, hills where tree-shaded bungalows climbed and looked down upon us. We could almost smell late breakfasts sizzling on stoves, and our pinched stomachs cried out eagerly to us. We couldn't wait to get ashore.

"You'll luf this country," said the affable second mate, leaning at the rail beside us. "The beer! Best in the vorld. The vimmen! I don't know about here, but in Sydney! By God, they trip you up and beat you to the ground, no?"

What he and Uncle Bim failed to mention was the trade unions. We coasted into the harbor and anchored. I suppose there must have been some radio conversation with the shore about a tug to ease us into our slip. But no tug approached. We stood on deck, packed and impatient, steaming in the heat. Nothing happened.

At last we got word that the wharf laborers were on strike and we'd have to stay out there until Australian troops could be rounded up to dock us and unload us. I remember a great wave of rebellion passing through the 300 of us. Spontaneously, as one man, we surged forward toward that off-limits deckhouse where the ground officers could sip gin under a fan, and we yelled our heads off. Mutiny on the slave ship! Glorious!

I don't know what that accomplished, though I still hope, all these years later, that those creased-pants bastards feared for their fat lives. Anyway, the captain, a Viking at heart, took the ship in himself and docked her, and we all pitched in to unload her. The "wharfies," lolling around the dock, yelled obscenities at us, and we yelled back, and then some Australian soldiers showed up—big, friendly guys in sloppy broad-brimmed hats—told the wharfies to bugger off, and got to work beside us. And so we emptied the ship and stepped ashore in Australia.

While we were aboard, daily routine had taken care of us. Now we were like prisoners suddenly released. We hadn't a clue what to do with ourselves. We wanted to wander through this strange place, to drink some of its fabled beer, to meet girls, above all to eat real food. But we were loaded with luggage and had no place to put it. We were pouring with sweat and had no showers to soak under. We had no home.

We turned toward our only first lieutenant, a pleasant man, one of us in every way except a shade more rank. Now was the time for him to use it, and we impressed this upon him, standing there on the dock near the snarling wharfies.

"The soldiers say there's a place here called Garbutt Field," he said. "Don't move an inch, and I'll phone them and round up some transportation."

We lolled in a patch of shade for more than an hour. It didn't seem long. We'd been lolling for a month. When our leader returned, he was riding in the first of half a dozen army trucks. They pulled up, and we all tried to cram ourselves in, bags and all, and of course each truck could take only about eighteen of us, so they had to make three trips to get us all to Garbutt Field. We couldn't see much on the way except dust, since the trucks were uncovered and the drivers delighted in going as fast as possible.

We disembarked, covered with grime, on a hot, dry field where caked red dirt was spotted by gray-green bushes. Some new barracks buildings rose from this desert like bleak islands, baking under the sun. In the distance, a mutter of aircraft engines added a familiar note and made us feel a little less forlorn.

At last, a young American officer appeared, looked us over in frank astonishment, and actually blushed.

"I really didn't know about you," he said. "Our communications are very bad, and this sort of thing has happened before—people arriving unexpectedly. But in this case—well, *three hundred* of you! I guess I can find a few tents, but...."

Tents? Then the barracks were full. We looked dubiously around at a number of enormous ant hills.

"How about some of us finding quarters in town?" Guppy asked. Trust Guppy to find a marvelously self-serving solution to every problem. There were murmurs of enthusiastic endorsement. The last thing we wanted, after those weeks on the troopship, was a military encampment. Especially here.

The embarrassed officer relaxed with a delighted smile. "Do you think you could? We'll see to it that you get paid tomorrow."

A rumble of approval. Townsville suddenly looked like paradise.

The trucks brought us back to the American military district office on a side street in the center of town. We piled out, agreeing to meet here each morning. We guessed word would come here if we were to be sent north. We didn't care. We just wanted to be rid of confinement and get something to eat.

Groups of us headed off in all directions to forage for housing. Steve and Guppy and I paused in the main street to absorb this first relaxed view of an Australian community: blazing afternoon sun; a broad street with sidewalks shaded by porticoes and awnings. Signs proclaiming a lottery; a smell of new leather, mixed with rotting vegetables; pleasant-looking people, dozens in uniform, passing, talking in a distinctive accent, voices surprisingly low, paying little attention to us.

Thirsty, we entered an open stall decorated with pictures of oranges, and realized that we were probably on the verge of scurvy. A young girl with a pretty smile poured us a sort of orangeade made with fresh oranges, and to our surprise accepted our American money. Nothing ever tasted so good.

We continued along the street, wonderfully colorful to us with its signs, its shops completely open on the street side, with boxes of fruits and vegetables protruding onto the sidewalk. One of these open shop fronts included a white cockatoo in a cage which yelled an unmistakable obscenity at every passer-by. The proprietor explained that the bird had been the mascot of an Australian army unit.

On one corner we discovered the North Queensland Club, paused to stare at it, and were abruptly asked in by a stout and friendly gentleman who was about to enter. That confirmed what the booklet had said about the Australian instant cordiality. No American civilian would have been so quick with an invitation.

We accepted, of course. A big, comfortable room upstairs: pool tables, oversized for playing something called snooker; a long and welcoming bar. The barman drew us a beer, wonderfully strong and nutty and brown. We'd never tasted anything like it.

Perhaps it was a member of the North Queensland Club who directed us to seek lodging on the hillside we'd seen from the ship. Or maybe we just headed in that direction because a hill was attractive to us after so many weeks at sea. Anyway, the first place we tried—a bungalow with a front porch raised on stilts—accepted Steve, Guppy, and me as tenants.

The Dunnes offered us a porch to sleep on—luxury after the ship. They charged us what seemed like a pittance—we would get our own meals in town—and we promised to behave ourselves and not wake them by roaring in, thunderously drunk, at four in the morning.

We kept that promise assiduously. We were overjoyed to be away from the ship, and from Garbutt, and to be sheltered by this couple. Mr. Dunne was tall, lean, sixtyish, with a slightly beaky nose and big-boned wrists, quiet and self-contained, retired at last after years of faithful employment in a state government job. She was a delight. Frizzy bobbed hair and thin-rimmed spectacles, carefully formal at first, to conceal a surging sense of humor and a quick affection for us. She had a son, and he was in the army, "in the Eighth Division—they were the ones in Malaya, you know—and I suppose he's a prisoner now, but he'll be fine. He'll come back to us." No other possibility dared intrude on her sturdy confidence.

As they got to know us, they often asked us to join them for a cup of tea. Cups of tea seemed to appear every time there was a pause in the conversation, and we quickly picked up the habit.

Actually, conversation didn't lag all that much. She had as many questions for us to answer as we had for her: Did we know any movie stars?

Of course not. We didn't even know anyone in the States who knew any movie stars. Does she see kangaroos and koalas?

Sometimes out for a drive with "the Dad" they'd see a kangaroo. She'd seen koalas in a zoo. How about gangsters in Chicago?

Gee, I guess they're there, all right. We read about them. Do you go out to the Barrier Reef?

We go to Magnetic Island sometimes. You should go, too. But it's not really part of the reef.

And so it went, as each nationality laid to rest various public impressions of the other. Not until we got to know the Dunnes really well did we spring the question that to us seemed obvious. "Hey, Mrs. Dunne, did your family originally come as...er...convicts?

She laughed in delight. "Oh my, I don't think so. Why, if we had, the Dad and I would be rich now, wouldn't we?" Then she thought for a moment and said, "I've wanted to ask you something, too. Do any of you have any red Indian blood?"

We were ashamed that we couldn't think of any.

Bored by the quiet Sundays of 1942 North Queensland, we even went to church a couple of times with our new family. They weren't much for it, they told us, but they liked to remind God about their son in the Eighth Division, when they could. A bit of help would be appreciated. We went along with them, and sang the hymns loudly and kept an eye peeled for girls. Not much luck. Oddly, I don't recall girls in Townsville. They were there, all right, but my thoughts were on the strangeness of this experience and the mystery of the next.

CHAPTER
TWO

DYSENTARY, DENGUE, AND SUDDEN DEATH

As it happened, the next was Charters Towers. A daylong train trip inched us the 250 miles, the train moving with painful deliberation, making long, unexplained stops at tiny depots with nothing around them but empty land. Bored to the verge of madness, we took to swarming out of the stiflingly hot carriages at every stop, having a cold beer at the depot bar (the train crew was always there), and then jogging beside the train to the next station. One way or another, all 300 of us managed to reach Charters Towers at more or less the same time.

I wonder what "CT" is like now. I recall the high slag heaps from its mines, the same covered sidewalks as Townsville's, an open-air movie where you sat in folding deck chairs and shoved aside a couple of goats that wandered up and down the aisles foraging for snacks. Huge fruit bats—"flying foxes"— would swoop above the flickering screen. During the day, they hung from the trees like coconuts.

Beyond the town, rolling fields, evenly stippled by gum trees, rose to small hills and ridges, then sank to dried stream beds, hidden in dark-green growth, then rose again to the distant horizon. Beyond that was more of the same, unending, barely touched.

Our camp, next to the airstrip, was as beautiful as all the rest of the country. But it damn near killed us. Again we were unexpected arrivals, unknown strangers unwanted in this area, and facilities had to be hastily contrived for us. One result was bad water. Another was the too-hasty assignment to us of an army doctor. He turned out to be an alcoholic, quite unable to cope with our inevitable dysentary or do anything about the cause. While his replacement was being found, and a fresh water supply tapped from the ground, the entire encampment sickened. I remember long lines of drooping figures waiting their turn at the latrines. I lost a lot of weight there.

At last, under a new medical staff, we snapped out of it, and started to fly. A number of shabby, mud-smeared P-39s had arrived from New Guinea just for our use. Guppy noted a Band-Aid pasted on one fuselage, peeled it off, and found a bullet hole. The big Allison engines, moreover, brutally used in combat, were very tired. Two quit in flight, and the men bailed out and returned to base. Another pilot, turning onto "final" to land, spiraled into the ground. He severed a leg and bled to death before anyone could reach him. That wasn't the plane's fault; he just thought he was good enough to make a low, slow turn, wheels and flaps down, and he was wrong.

Nevertheless we flew daily. A captain from a New Guinea squadron had been assigned to instruct us, but we swamped him with our numbers and our needs. Mostly he sent us up to teach ourselves the kind of maneuvering we imagined we might need to know.

He did, however, lead us on some low-level flights, the flat-out, tree-clipping buzz jobs that were totally forbidden back in the States. What a revelation that was. The Airacobra, with its 37-millimeter cannon poking out from the propeller shaft, was designed as a low-level, ground support plane. At last we were using it in its element, and we found we had perfect forward visibility and quick control at blurring speed. Joyously, we twitched around hills and down into valleys. Once a white cloud erupted under and around us as we flashed along at 300 knots. Cockatoos. Luckily, not one struck a plane.

There was little to do on days off, but we'd try to cadge a jeep and ride out into the countryside without quite getting lost. Sometimes we'd simply walk. Any car or truck passing would offer a lift and we'd accept eagerly. The civilians here— mostly elderly men and women—shared the unself-conscious friendliness of all isolated country people. We all responded to their warmth, but it was our fellows from midwestern farms, from Texas and Oklahoma and Arizona, who clicked effortless- ly with these Queenslanders.

Because of that easy meshing of cultures, we set up, with local help, an old-fashioned barbecue. We chipped in for a couple of sheep and roasted them over a deep-set fire. For me—effete easterner that I was—this cookout was a first. I almost fainted with hunger, watching and smelling that sauce- drenched meat sizzling on its spit. Nothing ever tasted so good.

"Ground school" consisted of briefings about what awaited us in New Guinea. Again, our captain was overwhelmed by our vast innocence and by our new exuberance now that health had returned. We would swarm into a big briefing tent, cracking jokes, bored and restless with training, and he'd eye us somberly and tell us to look at the men next to us, left and right. "In a couple of months," he would say, "one of you will be dead."

It was the old military shock treatment, and we'd mutter "bull" under our breaths. Yet all of us would surreptitiously glance right and left.

We gradually realized that the captain, barely older than the rest of us, dreaded the very words "New Guinea." To him, the place meant Japanese Zeroes hurtling out of the sun, guns blazing, pinning themselves on your tail and blasting you with cannon fire, no matter how you squirmed and wriggled to save your skin. I don't know what he'd been through in the islands, but he seemed to consider every Japanese pilot an ace, every plane marked by a red circle a killing machine. Flying against them was to be avoided, not taught.

"That's why he was assigned here," said Steve in a moment of blinding truth, as we sat in our tent one evening, playing cards. "It wasn't to teach us. It was because he's no damn good any more to his squadron and they had to get rid of him."

Guppy and I laid down our hands, and the three of us looked at one another, thinking of the implications. We'd all three been nicely brought up, well educated, and given superb instruction as military pilots. All our young lives we'd been made aware of our own importance. Now we weren't important enough even to rate proper combat training. The army had shoved us here because they'd run out of room at Townsville, had sent a war-weary pilot to supervise our flying in planes that should have been grounded. We were nothing. Zilch.

As we came to understand the captain's defeatism, we all paid less attention to him and simply tried to teach ourselves, there at Charters Towers. We babied those wretched planes carefully. Yet as we pretended to attack one another, we sometimes stressed them too far. I once flipped into half a snap-roll, and my entire plexiglass canopy came loose and slung itself sideways so that the screaming slipstream filled my cockpit. A small tornado whirled around me, scouring the floorboards beneath my rudder pedals, blinding me with debris: dried New Guinea mud that long ago rubbed off someone's boots; cigarette butts snubbed out by some addict who had been willing to risk his life by lighting up despite the fumes.

The plane crabbed sideways, faltering, but I wiped my streaming eyes and fought it back onto the ground. The mechanics reattached the canopy as best they could, and got it flying again that afternoon.

The captain's briefings about the invincible Japanese became a joke. We read paperback novels during his lectures. A ground officer, stationed with us while awaiting assignment as a squadron intelligence officer, volunteered to lead discussions about the progress of the war. We pilots, recalling college days, took part enthusiastically, welcoming the familiar conjectures and arguments. Then, in a sudden, unheralded display of genius, the U.S. Army designated Carl Jacobsen to teach us a little Pidgin English.

He was a big, bright, amiable, easygoing planter from Lae, New Guinea. He'd been there when Amelia Earhart had set out on the last, fatal leg of her round-the-world flight six years before. He'd barely escaped capture when the Japanese invaded. "We buried the family silver," he told us. "They've probably found it by now. But if they find my case of whiskey, I'll bloody well take it out of their hides."

Carl's task was to tell us young innocents from the States how to get along with the natives if and when we bailed out and were picked up by them. Today, Pidgin is an established language for Papua, and its written form is a lot harder to make out than my old scribbles, spelled phonetically. I noted that when native help came after we landed in our 'chutes, we were to say, "Me Number One man belong lik-lik balus. Balus belong mefella e buggerup finis." We'd chant this line after Carl, like second graders.

We loved it. We badgered Carl for more, and got tidbits like the plea to find a "man belong Sydney," the promise of "many mark" in payment, the threat to the untrustworthy— "You gaminem mefella, plenty trouble e come behind"—the words for food: "kai-kai"; milk: "su-su belong bullamacow"; and (for fun) piano: "big fella bokis e got teeth, you bangem e sing."

We loved Carl, plying him with questions about his life at Lae, about the invasion. I don't know if his course saved lives, but Carl saved our sanity and our morale. He was a fresh, strong breeze in an encampment that stank of fear.

The only time I tried Pidgin English was on the Papuan lad who ran the laundry for the squadron I joined. Approaching him with a bundle of dirty clothes, I suggested that he "washim lap-lap belong mefella."

"Sure," he replied. "Just leave it under that tree, lieutenant."

That happened surprisingly soon after Carl's classes. Abruptly, we were told to pack up and board trucks for Townsville. There we were billeted at Garbutt for a few days. We had no duties, and went out to Magnetic Island to swim. It was idyllic, but the shark guard, perched in a tower with a Lee-Enfield rifle, was a sobering presence. Steve and Guppy and I had time to call on the Dunnes. They hadn't yet heard from their son. They never did.

One evening we heard explosions, piled out of our barracks in the dark, and stumbled right into our first air raid. Searchlights scissored up to a tiny dot buzzing angrily in the black sky. Ack-ack blasted away at it, and we stood craning to watch the distant blossoms of exploding shells far overhead. Then we heard the whine and thump of shrapnel fragments raining around us, and hastily put on our new steel helmets. A sudden roar of gunfire only a few yards off sent us diving for the ground. It came from a pair of .50-caliber machine guns wielded by an eager gun crew. Their target was about two miles out of range, but it was great fun to open fire, so what the hell?

It seemed silly to take a Japanese air raid seriously after that one. But I soon did.

On a bright morning soon after that exciting night, we were stowed aboard various planes for the flight to Moresby. I found myself in a B-17, and squirmed forward to the bombardier's position in the nose. Through the plexiglass, I watched Garbutt's runway drop away, the coastal hills fall aside, the coral-spotted sea and storm-patched sky stretch endlessly ahead. Then at last I saw a dark smudge on the horizon—thick afternoon clouds boiling above the mountains of New Guinea.

We debarked stiffly into head-thumping heat. A number of trucks and jeeps pulled up beside the bomber, their shapes rippling in the heat waves. We moved to the shade of the wing, and stared out at corrugated iron roofs in the blinding sunlight, at a backdrop of brilliant green hillsides, of rich blue sky and dazzling white clouds. Every natural color was intensified, as though to remind us humans of how the world had looked before we came along and loused it up.

CHAPTER
THREE

A HOME AT LAST!

The names of six of us were called by a young sergeant in bleached khakis, red around the legs from ground-in mud. He wore a green Australian jungle hat, and was so skinny his scanty clothes bagged on him. In two jeeps and a truck for baggage, we were driven past sprawling villages of drab canvas, up and down sudden shady gullies and through hot fields of tall grass where lines of trucks were parked. The dirt road was so badly eroded and potholed that our jeep made heavy weather of it, yet traffic on it was incessant, mostly Australian trucks. Their camouflage was greener than our ubiquitous olive drab (o.d.).

At last we swung onto a muddy, deep-rutted lane that climbed toward a house of the kind we'd come to know in Queensland—square, low, with wide verandas on every side and a corrugated iron roof. It had no walls, just screening. We didn't realize how well we'd get to know this building, the "Farmhouse." It served as mess hall, meeting place, officers' bar, and briefing room, for the 41st Fighter Squadron of the 35th Fighter Group, Fifth Air Force, U.S. Army.

Flung together haphazardly this unit, suddenly my own, was almost literally sent flying off in all directions after the Japanese attack on Pearl Harbor, December 7, 1941. First the men were aimed at the Philippines, but the Japanese beat them there, invading those islands too quickly for the squadron even to make a landing. Then the 41st headed for the Dutch East Indies (now Indonesia), but again the Japanese were too quick, swarming through the islands, crushing the meager Dutch defense forces.

17

At last the unit veered south to Australia. Though the Japanese had invaded the neighboring islands of New Britain in January 1942, and New Guinea in March, Australia was still unbreeched, still a viable refuge. The squadron settled at last at an airfield in Bankstown, outside Sydney, for some much-needed combat training.

Life was fine in Bankstown—good food and quarters, and a squadron flat beside Sydney harbor for pilots to use on leave. Sydney was a revelation to our young men. Most of them came from the heartlands of America and had never seen a city larger than this one. They expected the New York coldness they'd read about, and were astonished that people treated them cordially. In some cases the treatment was more than cordial, for a number of young ladies, over the weeks, simply adopted the squadron.

These were educated young women, socially impeccable, far removed from the tarts who used to rise out of cracks in the pavement whenever an American naval vessel pulled into Sydney. These women had been encouraged to meet Americans at the various officers' clubs, to make them feel welcome and ease their homesickness. Inevitably, the girls found the Yanks, especially the pilots, a rather exciting lot— crude, yet glamorous; self-confident, yet wistfully uncertain— and relationships sprang up.

My bewildered squadron, numbed by constant moving, lacking any sense of cohesion, found this group of Sydney girls unbelievably attractive. Their national trait—the aura of clean healthiness and clear-eyed honesty—was very different from the game-playing American women a pilot would meet at, say, Selfrage Field, Michigan. Three years of war had made these Australians impatient with game playing and realistic about the very possible shortness of life. To my squadron mates, facing a scary future in New Guinea, they brought a radiant, delightfully refreshing interlude. In several cases, lasting marriages resulted.

The Bankstown era, in the first half of 1942, was a happy time for the squadron. Then came orders for New Guinea, and the pilots put on a farewell airshow for Sydney, starting as a disciplined formation flight and suddenly degenerating into wild excesses. They funneled under the Sydney Harbour Bridge like a swarm of bees. They all but lifted the roof off the squadron flat. They did victory rolls over Kings Cross. And Roger Heming, recognized as the most skillful among them, buzzed decorously businesslike Pitt Street inverted—"below the rooftops" swore other members of his flight. With this sort of thing out of their systems, the 41st came to Moresby, a band of brothers eager for combat. When they got it, they found they were outclassed.

The P-39 Airacobra was built by Larry Bell as a revolutionary fighter. She was a little plane—only a 34-foot wingspan—with a clean design and a fine, high-performance wing. Her cockpit was enclosed; you entered through a small door like that on your Ford sedan, back home. Her big Allison engine—about 1200 horsepower—was mounted behind the cockpit, with the drive shaft running forward on the keel of the fuselage, then hooking up with the propeller shaft through a gear drive. This allowed room for a 37-millimeter, or 20-millimeter cannon to be mounted above the drive shaft so that its muzzle passed through the hollow propeller shaft and protruded from the middle of the nose cone.

This cannon, along with four .30-caliber machine guns in the wings and two .50s synchronized to fire through the propeller, gave the 'Cobra pretty good firepower. That, and her sleek lines, made her a favorite with civilian "buffs," and advertising copywriters. She was hyped as a wonder plane, a product of Yankee ingenuity and know-how.

The icy fact was, all that armament added disastrous weight. The U.S. Army Air Corps, still thinking of her as a low-level ground support plane rather than a fighter-interceptor, denied her the two-speed supercharger she'd been designed for. So the graceful P-39 climbed sluggishly to about 20,000 feet and wallowed around up there without much enjoyment until her fuel gave out (pretty quickly), and down she came. Adding a belly tank gave her little more than a three-hour range, but cut her speed even more.

When the enemy attacked her—and according to their journals, they liked nothing better than to spot a flight of Airacobras—they'd swing down out of the sun from far above.

If a 'Cobra had height enough, she'd dive for the deck, for with her nose straight down, the plane could go almost as fast as her publicity claimed for her in level flight. But when caught at low altitude, with no more room for diving away, a '39 pilot could only jink around frantically to throw off the enemy's aim, and yell into his radio for help.

My squadron told the story of one such case, when fighter control at Moresby assured a desperate 'Cobra pilot that anti-aircraft guns would pick off his grim pursuer if the Yank could lead him over 7-Mile Strip. The Yank did so, the ack-ack opened fire—and shot down the P-39.

The fact that these new squadron mates of mine considered that episode pretty funny tells a lot about them. After too long a time of neglect, then too much joy in the Bankstown era, they'd faced too much war too suddenly. Battered by losses of friends, planes, and pride, they now eyed their duty with dour fatalism and death-row humor. We six replacements, ignorant of what was in store for us, and still enthusiastic about striking a blow for the American Way of Life, brought them a glimmering hope that six of them might be released from the sweltering tropics, from the bad and inadequate food, and from the shadow of death.

Beyond the Farmhouse, up the hill, was a clutter of tents, scattered without order among scrubby trees. Near the top were some empty ones, walls furled up to reveal a bare interior with dirt floor dry and gravelly, and cots with air mattresses and o.d. blankets folded on them under mosquito bars. Designed to hold four men, they had ample room for three. Obviously this squadron wasn't overpopulated.

We quickly chose our homes and chucked our bags inside. Steve and I shared a tent with Ben Briker, a scraggly Californian with a quick wit, a scratchy voice, and a gap-toothed smile. He'd been in our operational training unit in Florida, where we'd learned—more or less—how to get a P-39 into the air and land it again. The other replacements, Foxey Schriver, Willy Mcecham, and Doug Horochov, were next door. I don't think any of us cared where and with whom we would live; it was life itself that absorbed our attention just then.

But the sergeant noted our choices with a chewed pencil before driving us downhill, past the Farmhouse, off on another rutted lane that swung down beside an airstrip fashioned of steel matting. Planes were well hidden in revetments, but now that we were looking for them we could make out their topmost parts: the blade of a propeller, black with a buff-colored tip, the gleam of a rounded canopy, the gentle curve of a tail fin—only a P-39 had those graceful, feminine lines.

We whirled up to a small control tower, a little platform set perhaps 20 feet high on a frame of well-braced logs. Beside it, a rectangle of more logs held up a grass-thatched roof. Here we scrunched to a halt.

"Meet the squadron," said the driver. "The tall guy coming toward us is the C.O."

We scrambled out quickly. Our eyes, adjusting to the shade under that cool roof, took in a steel desk with a field telephone, one folding table smothered by books and papers, another holding a going game of Monopoly, a cracked schoolroom blackboard, a folding bulletin board shingled with pinned notices, and a row of canvas cots along one edge where a dozen thin young men, mostly stripped to the waist, lolled, sprawled, sat, slept, played bridge or solitaire, read paperbacks, wrote "V-mail" letters. The one approaching us wiped his sweat with a dark-green Australian army shirt, then put it on. It carried no insignia.

We'd been transient officers—unassigned to any squadron—for many weeks, and our nine-month gestation period as cadets had imprinted upon us certain military reflexes. We all straightened and started to salute. The man in the Australian shirt simply waved off the gesture. "You can forget that shit," he said, not unkindly. "Welcome to the 41st. I'd like to get you into the air as soon as possible, so John G. will lead you around, three at a time."

We were aware of a brief chuckle from the cots where the thin young men had all turned to look at us. John G. (as opposed—so we learned—to John E.) rose, zipped up a torn gabardine flying suit, and approached. Skinny, sweaty, prematurely bald, a wispy mustache. "You, you, you," he said, pointing, and I was one. "Parachutes are in the planes. Y'all look about the same size as the rest of us, so they'll fit. You'll get your own after we land, along with your other stuff. Come on. This jeep." And after waiting so interminably to belong to something, we suddenly did.

Hurry-hurry-hurry. I vaguely remember a sense of discomfort at the thought of using someone else's carefully fitted parachute, at not having a flying suit, a helmet, and goggles. Then I was dumped off at a revetment, and scrambling up the wing of a plane with the help of a crew chief in nothing but a pair of greasy hacked-off shorts, I suddenly realized that this aircraft was a glittering showpiece compared with the junk we'd been flying in Charters Towers. It was clean, beautifully maintained, and when I started the engine it sounded new and firm, no rattling vibration, no slap of loose valves.

I itched around in my straps to make them comfortable and slipped on the helmet and earphones hanging on the stick—slightly soggy with someone else's sweat, but no matter. John G. taxied out to the end of the strip, and with a roar was away, climbing and turning right. We followed in any old order, turning inside him to catch up and join formation.

The delight of flying again washed over me and relaxed me. The dense tropical air was quickly cooler and drier; the view down, at towering trees, clustered tents on ravaged hillsides, winding dirt roads, put everything into perspective. John G. led us around our strip—7 mile—so we could tell it from the many others that ribboned the area. He took us over the port, the old harborside buildings and docks, smeared by many an air raid. Below, the water was glassy and inviting. The southern coast of the island rumpled down to it in brilliant green hills and darkly shadowed inlets. Northward was a blue horizon climbing into a wall of towering clouds that boiled upward over the Owen Stanleys, spreading and blossoming as I watched.

John G. turned on a wing and sank into a shallow dive toward the bow of a sunken freighter protruding from the water. His voice scratched in my earphones: "Thirties only." I clicked the toggle switch for the four .30-caliber wing guns and turned on my gunsight, a circle of light on the armor-glass windscreen. When the plane ahead of me took its shot and peeled away, I centered the wreck and squeezed the trigger. Some froth in the water and a few ricochets from hits. Not very good shooting, but at least it was practice. I'd never shot any of the guns before.

Waggling his wings, John G. got us in close formation for landing. He swung widely toward the dip between hills where our strip lay, then lowered his nose and started to reach down, howling with speed, toward the trees and grassy ridges that flashed underneath. We formed an echelon on his left and slightly above him, as we'd been taught, then clung to him in astonishment as he got lower and lower. The steel matting blurred under us and I thought his prop must surely strike it. And then he was gone, up and to the right in a sweeping turn so violent that his wingtips left distinct condensation trails in the still, humid air.

We followed, one by one, urging our planes abruptly up and to the right—not beefing the controls, for that would cause this perverse little P-39 to snap-roll, but using the control pressure that came simply from the swing and roll of our bodies. That was enough to produce a turn that made my cheeks sag downward, my eyelids droop with the Gs.

I snapped down wheels and flaps and followed the pattern onto the strip. My wheels touched with a rattle and I felt good about the landing. But the C.O. wasn't impressed by any of us. After we'd turned the planes over to the next contingent, and presented ourselves again at the alert shack, he shook his head at us, sadly. "You guys have a lot to learn" was all he said.

What we had to learn was partly technique, and to me, at least, that came slowly but surely. The other part was attitude, and for a while I didn't think I'd ever achieve it. A fighter pilot, back then (and I think now, too), needed a capability for utter recklessness, a sudden zest for wild daring that he could switch on inside his head, then switch off again just in time to save his own life. I wasn't sure I had it, or that these old pilots would help me achieve it.

For we realized, listening to their talk, that they had shared things we could never know. The squadron had been hurled into the New Guinea skies in the effort to snatch control of the air away from the Japanese. Dive-bombing and strafing, the enemy had slashed at the Aussie ground troops who were struggling to win back the Kokoda Trail over the mountains; our job had been to supply at least a little aerial competition for the Zekes and the Oscars—army-type Zeroes, built by Nakajima—which escorted the Japanese bombers, Lilys and Bettys and Sallys, that pulled off devastating raids.

These thin, ivory-colored young guys had done the best they could with planes that a halfway competent Japanese fighter pilot could shoot down almost at will. And the squadron had taken its losses hard, perhaps because of all the men had shared.

We heard about the squadron's beginnings, the early days, the Bankstown era, bit by bit in the weeks that followed. We began learning about New Guinea that first evening when, after drawing parachutes, Mae Wests (inflatable life jackets), Colt .45 automatics, shoulder holsters, and flying suits, we repaired to the Farmhouse to join the "old" pilots. I was in a sober frame of mind because of my flying suit, a clean, gabardine one-piece coverall, a little small for me. I liked it because of its soft feel, and because the small size erased all bagginess. When I made a move in the cockpit, I didn't want any bulge of fabric to hinder me. But I queried the supply officer about its well-worn look—including a few small tears.

"Yeah, it belonged to Wilder," he answered. "We got it off him when he bought the farm. But Jerry washed it twice, so it's all clean."

I knew Jerry was the squadron's Papuan laundry boy, but I had no idea who Wilder was or what had happened to him. Perhaps wearing his suit was bad luck. Yet I realized that if I was going to let that sort of thing rule my life here, I might as well just go out and crash on takeoff. I took the suit, and over the months it became no longer Wilder's, but mine, bending itself to my body, thinning out under the wear of my straps, my buckles, my bony shoulders. What luck it brought me was good. I lived.

That first evening, around the bar at the Farmhouse, the old guys treated us with awkward friendliness. They wanted us to feel appreciated, to find, perhaps, a hint or two of pleasure in the squadron's life, so that we wouldn't simply abandon all hope. Having surreptitiously watched our landings, the veterans, I was later told, inwardly groaned at all we had to learn, and tried to ease us into a slight grasp of what to expect.

"You'd better just drink some of this squash," said John G., making room for me. "You and I are doing a weather flight tomorrow."

I looked up, questioningly.

"Nothing to it," he said. "We just fly up to the target area, call in the weather, then fly back. If the weather's OK, the mission will be on its way by the time we land. Just stay with me and keep your eyes open and your head turning."

I nodded, gulping a lemony drink, minus alcohol. Obviously, the best way for us to learn was to go straight to work.

After a fairly miserable dinner—"bully beef à la Yellow Flight," explained an old pilot named Otto Kelvin, who had established himself as a minor wit—I found myself not only posted for the weather flight, but selected as tonight's officer of the guard. This was nuisance duty for the newest officers, a matter of periodically checking the sentries to see if they were awake. I had to know the current password, so the sergeant of the guard revealed it: "Wooloomooloo."

"What in hell is that?" I asked.

"A place in Sydney," he said. "The Nips can't say it. They can't say 'L'."

"Are there really any Nips around here?"

"Beats me, lieutenant. But they sure know everything we know."

Guard duty went fine. I slept in my clothes, and the sergeant nudged me awake twice, and I managed to say "Wooloomooloo" at the right moments, and all the sentries were cheerfully awake. Then I slept for a very short time before being roused by a watchman's rattle outside the tent and the voice of the C.Q. (charge-of-quarters): "First flight! First flight!"

I stumbled out of my mosquito bar in the pitch dark and fumbled for my flying suit. Steve turned on a flashlight. "Shake it first," he said. "Someone told me always to shake your clothes before you put them on. And bang your boots to get out the scorpions."

"Scorpions!" I exclaimed. I banged heel-first, and shook the boots. Something popped out and scuttled away. "Jesus!" I said. "I think I had one. Why aren't you asleep?"

"Hard to sleep. I'm on next call, anyway. So's Ben."

"Good luck," I said.

"You, too."

In the blackness I felt my way downhill to the Farmhouse and found lights blazing inside the blackout curtain. A cook waved me to a place at one of the long wooden tables where the enlisted men ate. Officers' Mess didn't exist until dinnertime, when we got one table nearest our barroom.

I fetched a plate of breakfast. "French toast" was a slab of white bread with a greasy, half-cooked slice of bacon laid on top. You could smear the whole thing with waxlike imitation butter and then add "syrup," which was simply water and sugar boiled together. The coffee was wonderful.

John G. came in, nodded, and silently picked at his food. "Our call sign is 'Beaver,'" he suddenly said, between sips of coffee. "And this sector is 'Maple.' We'll get the codes for the weather at the alert shack. They change all the time. Keep looking around when we're in the air. Don't just stare at me to hold formation. Spread out and look everywhere, especially above and behind. Oh, and 'Angels' means altitude. If sector tells us to go to 'Angels Twenty,' we try like hell to get up to 20,000 feet. In these planes it ain't easy."

I realized John G. wasn't used to briefing new pilots. He was telling me things that were as natural to him as breathing.

In the distance we could hear the rumble of engines being preflighted by the crew chiefs. We downed our cups and rose. I felt a nervous twitch in my innards.

"Latrine?" I asked.

"At the flight line. We'll have time there."

We mounted a jeep and rattled away. There was still no sign of the sky lightening in the east, but as we neared the line we saw flashes of blue light from the revetments—exhaust flames from the running up of the engines. I'd been permanently assigned to Red Flight. Its planes were all in the 70s or 170s, and I'd been given Number 74 to fly. We drove past it and I looked at its flame critically, as if my life depended on it. As far as I could tell, it looked fat and lively.

My tension mounted. After a hasty visit to the latrine, I drew my parachute from the tent where they were kept and lugged it to the plane. The crew chief helped me set it in the deeply dished seat, straps opened so I could quickly worm into them. I put my helmet and goggles over the top of the control stick, then hung my Mae West on the open door. With only my shoulder holster strapped around my flying suit, I jumped down and went back to the shack. That was the first time I went through that procedure—which would become part of my life—and I remember it well.

It was quiet and dark in the shack, with just three of us—two pilots and the operations clerk, a young sergeant with a Louisiana accent, busily writing up a report. John G. showed me the day's weather code: "Tiny" meant OK to fly the mission; "Dancer" meant socked-in. He tossed me a blue pamphlet. "Intelligence report," he said. "Read it when we get back. The Jap diaries are pretty interesting."

He looked at his wristwatch and rose. "Let's get 'em into the murk. Remember to look around." We went out to his jeep. I could feel my pulse beating inside my ears—too fast—and was annoyed by my rapid breathing. My innards roiled. It was like waiting for the curtain to rise on the school play I'd starred in. No, it was worse than that.

John G. dropped me beside my revetment and I scrambled onto the dew-damp wing of Number 74, getting a hand from the waiting crew chief. I was ashamed to be so nervous on this first, simple, relatively safe mission. But I sensed I was starting a new life—which might well be a short one.

Settling into the cockpit, I fumbled for parachute straps and was helped by the crew chief. I snapped the lead from my earphones into the radio and suddenly the outer sounds of engines running up were muffled and I entered that special realm of intimacy that the radio seemed to bring, the crash of static, quickly tuned down, the occasional murmur of voices on fighter frequency. John G.'s came in loudly: "Maple, from Beaver Special: How do you read? Over."

"Beaver Special, you are R five, S five. Over."

"Roger, Maple. Out."

As a wingman, I didn't have to do that radio check. But I felt the imminence of takeoff, and was disturbed to see the sky still totally dark. My experience in night-flying a P-39 amounted to exactly zero. Yet, sure enough, here came a dark shadow rumbling past my revetment. John G. was taxiing out. Apparently I was about to roar off the ground with him, in utter blackness, and for the first time ever, in tight formation.

The crew chief touched my knee, and I nodded at him, snapped on switches, and pressed my heel down on the energizer. He closed my door and jumped off the wing as the slow whine of the starter rose in pitch to a scream. I rocked my foot forward, pressing my toes on the engager. The 12-foot propeller jerked around before me, and I added a shot of prime. With a bark and a blast the engine caught. Yellow flame rippled from the exhaust stacks behind me, then turned to a steady blue glow as the Allison smoothed out. I raised a gloved hand to the crew chief and he half-saluted in the old tradition. I eased off the brakes and let the plane roll forward after John G.

It was then that I realized that I had been able to see my propeller turn; I had seen the crew chief's salute. With timing that seemed uncanny, but that we all quickly learned to judge, I was headed for takeoff at the very first flicker of visibility in this land without half light. By the time John G. and I had lined up, checked our magnetos, waggled ailerons back and forth to show readiness, and finally poured on the coal and lifted off the strip, the sun was a blazing sliver in the east, and its rays fanned across the high clouds to form a giant Japanese flag. An uneasy omen if ever there was one.

CHAPTER FOUR

MY LIFE AS A BEAVER

Takeoff in that damp, heavy air, cool from the night, was smooth as glass. Condensation trails formed at every contour of our planes—wingtips, antennae, air intake, rudder tip. John G.'s prop carved neat white spirals behind him, and when he snapped up his wheels on liftoff the contrail ribboned from them, then suddenly snapped off as the landing gear doors closed.

I held formation with him as he turned on course—due north—and then slipped a bit away, trying to find the right separation for a wingman, the spot where I could look around safely, yet still read what I could see of the element leader's face through his goggles and oxygen mask. Finding position, more or less, I tried to hold it, to keep my speed exactly right, to anticipate John G.'s turns and slide under him so I wouldn't move ahead. I was his satellite, attached to him as though by gravity, first off his right wing, then his left wing, then right again.

On my first crossover, I lined up the blur of his propeller through the arc of my own. When you did this, an image would form of three propeller blades turning slowly to the right or left. By adjusting your own rpms, you could make those ghostly blades stand still. That meant that your rpms were exactly the same as the leader's. It was a nice trick—one I learned at Charters Towers—and it soon became as instinctive as unlocking my shoulder harness so I could twist my body around in the cramped little cockpit.

We climbed gently in the sunrise. To my right I looked down at a dark carpet of jungle rising to velvety foothills deep-etched by the low sun. They climbed to the great peaks of the Stanleys, abrupt cliffs and overhangs, the sawtooth horizon of a relatively newborn range. The peaks seemed impossibly high at first, but when my swinging head and searching eyes returned to them, they'd slipped below the horizon and revealed the sea beyond—off the north coast of the island—blazing gold in the sunlight.

We were headed toward Wau, where an airstrip had been fashioned in the floor of a narrow valley, a canyon, really, adjoining the Bulolo gold fields. The Japanese were determined to capture the strip, and then the gold, and were scrambling over the mountains from the Salamaua Peninsula, gathering strength for a push that would overrun the Australian defenders. C-47 cargo planes, heavy with supplies and Aussie infantry, staggered to Wau every day, and our job was to keep the convoys from being attacked. Since New Guinea weather played a major role in any aerial mission, John G. and I were off to judge the prospects for today.

I kept my head turning, all right, but I didn't yet know how to look. When you scan a seemingly empty sky with your eyes focused for infinity, you instinctively expect to see nothing, and that's what you find. Your brain often refuses to note what there is. Fighter pilots of my day, dependent on eyes alone, learned to shift mental gears to accept the fact that somewhere in that bright emptiness lurked tiny dots. Then, believing in them, you began to see them—*there!* About 45 degrees above that mountain peak—*There!* Right below the edge of that cumulous cloud—*There!* Straight above: "Twelve o'clock high!"

I read as a boy that World War I pilots learned to block out the sun with a thumb and look around it. Soon I was doing the same thing. The sun has always been the hiding place for the enemy.

On this first mission I kept looking, faithfully, but blindly, as we chugged northward over pink-tinged crests and deep, black valleys wreathing with the mists of early morning.

Looking down into that wilderness, a lost world from primordial times, I wondered what would happen if an engine quit.

And, of course, my engine instantly began to run rough, hammering unevenly at me through my padded earphones. Grimly, I accepted the prospect of bailing out. I checked my parachute straps and eyed the red release lever on the door. Pull that, and it would shuck off the hinges and let the door fly off. Then you were supposed to roll out so your shoulder would hit the wing. If you hit the wing, so they said, you wouldn't be struck by the tail.

I was more or less resigned to leave the plane. But the engine didn't get any worse, and pretty soon I forgot about it. On every mission I flew over the Owen Stanleys from then on, my engine ran rough. That was just the way of it.

John G.'s voice suddenly scratched in my ears: "Clear your guns."

I'd been told about this. If the guns got too cold, flying as we were at 16,000 feet, the breech mechanism would fail. A little burst would warm them up. I snapped on the gun switches and tuned in my sight. Then I touched the trigger on the stick.

A sharp rasp of machine guns and two thumps from the cannon. I'd never fired it before. Its heavy vibration, almost under my spread legs, gave me a sense of extraordinary potency. And then, directly in front of me and right at our altitude, two puffs of dark brown smoke blossomed in midair.

I jogged quickly up and away from John G. and squeezed my microphone button. "Ack-ack!" I gurgled.

We wore throat microphones back then, and if you didn't hold them against your Adam's apple while you spoke, your words were just squawks. But John G. understood what I said and reacted with remarkable coolness. "Those are your own shells," he drawled.

And of course I then remembered that if 37-millimeter shells failed to blast their target, they'd explode anyway after a short interval. Sheepishly, I snuggled back into position. John G. barely glanced over at me. He never mentioned my little gaffe.

At last we approached a pass over the mountains, and flew into it. Beyond, a valley twisted between smaller mountains. The area had a different look to it, a hint, perhaps, of meager settlement. But we didn't go farther. We slid into a broad turn, 180 degrees, and my leader's southern voice came in: "Maple, this is Beaver Special. Go ahead, Maple, this is Beaver Special."

And then a distant voice, Australian: "This is Maple. Come in Beaver Special."

"Maple from Beaver Special. Tiny. Tiny. Tiny. Do you read, Maple?

"Beaver from Maple. Read you tiny tiny tiny."

"Roger Maple. Beaver out."

Abruptly we were headed home, the sun now on our left, and high enough to reveal the mysterious bottomlands in those dark valleys, lush and green, with often the silver glint of a stream. Now, as we passed over this bad country, my engine ran sweetly, and I relaxed, enjoying the flight, looking around only cursorily.

When John G. rocked his wings slightly and pointed straight up, I was mortified to see a distinct contrail headed north, far above, against the dark blue of the sky. I drew closer to John G. and looked at him for some sign. He nodded his head, slightly. That was the enemy, all right. Now what? Were we supposed to struggle up toward it? The damn thing must be at 40,000 feet, twice as high as we could reach.

My leader simply flew straight on, course due south for Moresby. I got back to my position and renewed my watch with fervor. If that plane had been headed down toward us, a lot of help I'd have been.

We lowered our noses and coasted down from the mountains to the flatlands and swamps that reached south to the port. My eyes burned with the effort of seeing planes. And then abruptly, there they were, a flight of C-47s with P-39s weaving above them—our squadron. We passed 10,000 feet apart, we low, they high.

John G.'s voice: "Beaver leader from Beaver Special. Have fun."

And the answer: "Beaver Special, we've got you. Out." Which meant either that the leader saw us or agreed with us about having fun, or both.

On the ground, John G. and I jeeped to the almost empty alert shack. He was relaxed and friendly, the pressure off him, the job done for today. I felt that my flying was about what he expected. He wasn't overjoyed with me, but he wasn't especially displeased either. I was an average greenhorn.

"What about that Jap plane?" I asked as we sipped a cup of green limeade known as "battery acid."

"That was a Dinah," he said. "It's the only thing that could get that high. Probably unarmed. They use them to take pictures. We see them often, and I guess they see us, and we just leave each other alone. But you should have spotted it."

"I know," I said.

"Heading home is the hard time," he said. "We all tend to stop looking. And that's when the bastards bounce you."

I sprawled on a cot with the blue book and read an assessment of a captured Oscar, the Japanese Army Ki-43, a Zero-type fighter. Amazingly maneuverable, wrote the test pilot, but we should be able to handle it if we hit and run in a shallow dive.

Fine, but we'd have to get higher in order to dive, and we had P-39s that had problems getting higher than a duck. I fell asleep for a while, then rolled upright on the cot and dealt a hand of solitaire. I was still trying to come out when there was a roar that shook the roof, and I went out to watch the returning flights buzz the strip and peel up for their landings. All the belly tanks were on, so presumably they hadn't tangled with the Japanese.

Soon the pilots were with us, faces grimy with ground dust that had stuck to sweat except where their goggles had been. Steve looked both tired and exhilarated. "How was it?" I asked.

"Okay, I guess. Long. Hard work. How was yours?"

"Not as long. Hey, we saw a Nip."

"The hell you did. Did you get him?"

"He was about four miles above us—a Dinah. Taking pictures." I felt very important.

"What did he look like?"

"A contrail," I admitted.

Someone called out "Smoko!" and we all gathered at the tailgate of a battered truck where coffee was ladled out in tin cups. I added sweetened condensed milk, and stirred it. A small cluster of brown ants rose to the surface and I tipped them out, then hesitated about whether or not to drink the rest.

"Go ahead." Roger Heming, the guy who'd allegedly buzzed Pitt Street upsidedown, was watching me sardonically. "Ants don't drink much."

"After six months here, you'll gulp 'em right down," said another old pilot—Peter Fletcher, a short, blond midwesterner who would have been stocky if this hadn't been New Guinea.

"After a year here, if you don't have ants in your coffee you'll scratch around and get some." That was Otto Kelvin, a Californian with pale blue eyes.

"A year! Hell, Kelvin, you ain't even been here four months!" My friend John G. from Tennessee was unmistakable. Kelvin and three others had indeed joined the squadron as the earliest replacements, having trained in Canada with the RCAF. I would soon admire the wealth of dirty songs they'd acquired there.

Coffee cups clanged on the bed of the truck as we tossed them in. I looked at the group of us, including myself. Sixteen Army Air Forces pilots in at least a dozen uniforms. Most of us were bare to the waist, but the few shirts were wonderfully varied: an issue sun-tan with the sleeves cut off at the shoulders, a blue workshirt stenciled "U.S. NAVY." A white T-shirt proclaiming "Perdue Athletic Assn."

Most khaki pants had been hacked into shorts with hunting knives. Flying suits, generally unzipped and tied around the waist, varied from olive drab gabardine to suntan cotton. One was blue—a trade with some RAAF pilot. Several of the old pilots wore the beautiful, fleece-lined RAAF flying boots.

The mission was over for the day. One look to the north explained why: Cumulus clouds were boiling over the mountains, shouldering their way higher and higher toward the stratosphere. No more planes could get into Wau until tomorrow.

I entered 1 hour and 30 minutes in my logbook, and Steve, sitting on an adjacent cot, wrote 2 hours and 25 minutes in his. We found books to read. We were on alert for the rest of the day, ready to scramble if the Moresby fighter sector picked up radar blips that acted more like a formation of planes than a thunderstorm.

The heat built up. Some of us played softball desultorily, dripping with sweat at every movement. The armament officer appeared, a tall, athletic man named Sheehan, to tell us that one of the planes was going to be bore-sighted. Don't panic if we heard a few shots.

Then Barnaby, the engineering officer, entered the alert shack and we new replacements, extra sensitive to every possibility, took notice. We'd met "Barney" at the Farmhouse bar the night before—a small, intense man who, according to the C.O., ran his division so well that the squadron had one of the best records in New Guinea for planes on flying status. When Barney said a plane could fly, it could. If he pulled it off the line, it needed pulling.

This time he spoke to Fletcher, the leader that day of White Flight. Fletcher nodded, then called out, "Bouchet! Want to slow-time eighty?"

Steve and I looked at each other in puzzlement, but Georges Bouchet (he carefully saw to it that the name was pronounced "Bouchay") downed his cards and rose from a bridge game. "For once, I had a winner," he said, in the flat tones of New England.

Another player turned the hand over. "Get out of here, Canuck," he said. "You had nothing."

Bouchet wormed his arms into his flying suit, zipped it up, donned his shoulder holster, and turned to Barnaby. "How long?" he asked.

"An hour. And keep the rpms down."

The two left together, and soon we heard an Allison engine sputter to life and roar with fresh vigor. Then there was the fading snarl of a '39 taking off, and Steve and I looked at each other again with at least some comprehension. From the sound, plane Number 80 had a new engine. It was getting a break-in, a "slow-time" flight. All was explained.

But not quite all. We noticed the old pilots glancing at one another, then gathering cards and—in the case of the eternal poker game—loose money, and stashing them in a steel box. One of them peered out from under the thatched roof.

"Here comes Canuck," he said. "Watch out!"

We all rose to look, and the older hands clutched their books and magazines to their bodies. Far away, beside the strip, a dark blob appeared low in the sky. It got big very quickly, and turned into the front view of an Airacobra heading straight for our shack, so low that dust plumed behind it.

No sound reached us until a half-second before the plane did, slashing over the roof with a shattering roar, sending scraps of thatch flying. As Bouchet pulled up, a tornado of slipstream tore through the shack, picking up every loose article and whipping it into a small tornado. I wiped dust from my eyes, found the cover of my paperback had blown off, then peered out the other side of the shack to see where the plane had gone. No sign of it. Just a distant rumble, high in the sky.

The pilots shook their heads and restored their cards and money and magazines. "That damn Canuck," someone murmured. That was all.

So the hot, sweaty afternoon passed. Canuck returned, and one pilot grumbled that he was a bastard, and he smiled innocently. A massive mountain of cloud finally reached up and blocked out the sun, and blessedly the heat eased. The possibility of a scramble faded with it. Moresby was suddenly better protected by the weather than by us. Nothing could get through those thunderheads. The old pilots wandered out to a framework of logs that held a 110-gallon belly tank. Its bottom had been pierced for a short length of hose with a homemade shower head screwed into it.

One by one the men stripped and showered. We replacements came last. "We've been here longer than you-all," John G. explained, kindly. "We stink worse."

Then we were in a jeep, bouncing back to the tents. I found a pair of khakis, a little cleaner than my shorts, and a shirt. And I hurried to the Farmhouse, anxious for a drink and some bully beef, however disguised, before I fell asleep on my feet.

C H A P T E R
F I V E

THE ROAD TO WAU

M y name was on the posting for the next day's Wau mission: Number Two in Red Flight, flying Herkimer's wing. So I was up again at first call with Ben. Steve got to sleep another hour.

I had a chance to talk to Joel Herkimer before takeoff, and immediately liked him. He came from Iowa, a thoughtful, instinctively friendly country man. I wanted badly to do well with him. "Keep looking around," he said, inevitably. "Don't just stare at me." Then he thought for a moment, and added. "Look at the edges of clouds. Where there aren't clouds, pretend there are." It was his private trick of learning to see, and it was typical of him to share it. The man was a born teacher.

The flight was like yesterday's weather hop, except an hour longer. Weaving above the lumbering transports, we seemed to take forever to get anywhere. But flying with 15 others added a gratifying sense of formidability. Surely no enemy would attack this array of machine guns and cannon.

None did as we followed the course to Wau, past the same mountains and deep valleys, where my engine suffered the same asthma, on into the same pass and this time through it to the three-walled valley, its floor smeared by the gravelly little airstrip that Japan wanted so badly.

Circling above, occasionally glancing down at the C-47s, landing and taking off, one after another, in a seemingly endless process, I realized that the strip at Wau had been patched on a hillside. That bottomland was a slanting ramp leading up into the closed end of the valley. The big planes slowed quickly as they trundled uphill. But after they'd turned around and spilled out their cargoes of men and gear, they'd get rolling so fast that the pull of gravity was obvious. They were off in no time, leaping eagerly into the air almost as though the airstrip were a ski jump. They seemed glad to be rid of all that weight and anxious to get out of this hostile place.

So was I. The sense of hostility was strong, and my eyes searched the sky almost, but never quite, seeing spots beside the clouds—real or, like Herkimer's, imagined. I willed myself to see enemies coming in. I tried to picture them—sleek, silvery, with scarlet circles splashed on their wings and perhaps jazzy hash marks slashing across their fuselages. I didn't know. I'd never seen a Japanese plane except for a bright spot in the searchlights of Garbutt Field, and that contrail yesterday with John G.

We orbited at 5000 feet, around and around the Wau strip, and though I'd been warned to switch from belly tank to main after an hour and 40 minutes, I forgot. My engine quit cold, and I experienced what other careless pilots have—the explosive impact of silence. As my plane dropped behind, my hand flew to the selector valve and twisted it, and since the prop was still wheeling, the engine caught with a roar and I was back on Herkimer's wing in four or five seconds.

But of course he'd noticed. He made a twisting motion with his gloved hand, and I nodded, and he seemed to shake his head in despair. For the first of many times I tried to picture whether it would be possible to make an emergency landing in a P-39 at Wau. It was a very short strip, but the 10-degree slant would help. Yet you'd have to be exactly right as you made your approach, dead stick. Even under power, no plane could go around for a second try. The wreck of a C-47 that had tried it scarred the hillside, a sobering reminder.

Today, half a century later, when I come awake for no reason in the middle of the night as old men do, I wonder about landing a fighter at Wau. I'm pretty sure I'd never have been able to make it. I'd have been better off bailing out and taking my chances with the jungle and the Japanese.

My moment of silence was my only problem on that first combat mission, and after we landed Herkimer kindly remarked that everyone forgot the belly tank at one time or another. It had no gauge, so you had to judge its fuel by the time. On every mission, it had to be used up first so it could be dropped if necessary. We took off on main tank, then switched to belly tank, then switched back to main at the right time.

While I'd been bumbling through that long buttock-cramping mission, the Fifth Air Force was earning kudos for the Battle of the Bismarck Sea. Since it boasted an airdrome, the town of Lae, on New Guinea's north coast, had been one of the first places seized by the Japanese. They'd been using it as the base for air attacks on Moresby, and the Allies, in turn, had been bombing it steadily to slow up those attacks.

We'd apparently succeeded in making life pretty uncomfortable, because at this moment a big Japanese convoy was heading across the Bismarck Sea for Lae, bringing supplies and reinforcements. Allied planes had spotted them. General George C. Kenney, Fifth Air Force commander, alerted his few squadrons of A-20s and B-25s, and when the weather cleared these attack planes and medium bombers, along with a flock of RAAF Beauforts and Beaufighters, found the convoy and clobbered it. A handful of P-38 (Lightning) squadrons got into the act. Our P-39s lacked the range for this strike, and I was glad of it, feeling, on that particular day, anything but "combat-ready."

There wasn't much combat in the Battle of the Bismarck Sea. It was mostly a massacre. Kenney had been stressing the technique of skip-bombing—attacking ships with bombs dropped low enough so that they skipped on the water like flat stones. The idea was an old one: Bombs exploding close beside ships cause a surge of water pressure that ruptures hulls. Skipping the bombs was a good way to accomplish this, and two months later British Lancasters used the technique on the famous "dam-buster" raid in Germany.

In the Bismarck Sea, skip-bombing worked fine. Japanese transports and their escorts capsized and sank right and left as the bombs blasted them near their water lines. Sailors and troops were spilled into the sea and swam about, clinging to floating wreckage, and, in one of the more unpleasant moments of the war, our planes strafed them until the water turned crimson. Then, presumably, the sharks took over.

I read now that we had hardly any casualties, but I know of one. He was with me back in Florida, a nice fellow and a good fighter pilot. Then he left us in Australia to join a B-25 squadron. He didn't care what he flew—he just wanted to get into it.

So he was over the Bismarck Sea, that day, and he bombed and then strafed the human flotsam in the reddening waves, churned by bullets. And he flew back and landed, and got out of his plane, and walked a little distance off. And he finally found a use for that big old awkward Colt pistol he had to carry. He put the muzzle in his mouth and blew away his brains.

On my first day off, I slept as late as I could, then for the first time Steve—also off-duty—and I unpacked our gear and stowed it in the tent, banging a few nails into the tent pole to hang clothes on. Steve joined a couple of other pilots who'd commandeered a jeep. They set off to explore the Moresby area.

Tired of my own smell, I visited Jerry with a small mountain of laundry. He was a mission boy, affable and bright, handsome and energetic, always devotedly plunging clothes into his giant copper kettle, shoving them around in boiling water with a heavy stick, then hanging them to dry. My shirts and pants came back tastefully faded and carefully folded to show the creases, and I put them neatly in my footlocker, and was proud of momentary tidiness. But I continued to wear only my cutoff shorts.

During much of my day off, I explored a collection of battered paperbacks in the Farmhouse, finding some good recent novels and three Shakespeare plays. Notices and cartoons cut from magazines were pinned on a makeshift bulletin board—a slab of plywood from a packing case. Four letters were displayed there, each containing much the same message:

Dear So-and-so,

You are such a good friend and we have meant so much to each other that I know you will understand when I tell you that I am going to marry Joseph, the man I work with at the factory—I'm sure I told you about him—next Tuesday....

Even "Dear John" letters weren't sacred with these tough, weary, isolated men.

I selected something to read, and sat down. After a while I went back to the empty tent to write some letters. I wrote, napped, read, visited other tents, chatted with other off-duty pilots, explored the sprawling campsite, looked for good things to eat with no luck, and at last recognized the fact that I was bored stiff. To my amazement, I missed the excitement of flying a mission. Hard to believe. Perhaps I was becoming addicted to the rush of adrenalin.

All day the sounds of aircraft engines rumbled in the distance—flights returning, some our own, bombers getting back from their strikes, engines being run up, an occasional fighter twisting through acrobatics high in the sky, perhaps being slow-timed, perhaps simply giving some ranking pilot a bit of fun. Right on time, the clouds built up, their shade cutting off the savagery of the heat.

Anxious for exercise, I walked to the flight line and slipped into the alert shack. I felt astonishingly at home under that thatched roof, amid those half-naked bodies. A few of my squadron mates glanced up at me as I edged over to Ben, who had flown that day. "How was it?" I asked.

"Nothing happened," he said. "We just flew up and stooged around and flew back. It's a long mission, though. I didn't think it would ever end."

"Did you remember to switch tanks?"

"Of course. I'm not a jerk, like some people."

Guthrie, the squadron operations officer, glanced over at me from his table. "Park, I'm putting you on Heming's wing tomorrow," he said. He was an aloof old-timer with thousands of hours and three enemy planes to his credit. I hadn't realized he knew my name. I nodded at him, my stomach automatically twisting a little at the knowledge that I was back in it. Yet the addiction was still there, all right. For I craved the mission as much as I feared it.

The pilots would soon call it a day, and I wanted to walk back up to camp instead of thumbing a ride in a jeep. I looked around once more at the cots and deck chairs, the quiet young men bending over their cards and books and the one weary Monopoly board. I was one of them, and I liked the feeling.

I didn't know, of course, that flying Heming's wing would render some considerable changes in me.

I have no idea how old Roger Heming was. The face was as unlined as a ten-year-old's: a keen, thin face with high cheekbones and a perpetual strand of straight blond hair sloping across the forehead. But the eyes belonged to a man of 60—pale blue eyes that had seen it all before and had grown tired of it, whatever it was. Heming seldom smiled. He always seemed remote, unconcerned with the rest of the squadron.

He didn't talk much—no torrent of hilariously vulgar stories poured from him as it did from Kelvin, for example. He took little part in the murmured conversations of the alert shack. When he did speak it was in the flat accent of the upper midwest, where all those Swedes had settled. Minnesota, probably.

What he said was remarkable only for its underlying cynicism. Heming hated a lot of specific things: food, heat, and discomfort among them. Actually, he loved only one thing: flying. Anything that got in the way of flying he hated. He hated a good deal of his life.

He'd been in the squadron forever—since it was first formed from the breakup of an old "pursuit" group. He'd joined up to fly, and that was his only ambition—not marriage and a family, not wealth and rank. Just flying whatever the U.S. Army shoved under his buttocks.

I'd noticed his long silences, his rather acid tongue when he did converse. I'd also felt that he was antagonistic to us new replacements. I hadn't realized just how deeply his dislike of us went until the next morning when we took off. Heming led Red Flight that day, and that meant he led the squadron. We two were the first off. We'd gotten a good, early start—the sudden morning light had barely arrived before we were cramming the throttles forward and feeling the acceleration push us back in our seats.

I rolled down the runway on Heming's right wing, moving my throttle forward smoothly, holding position, watching that plane on my left, barely ahead of me, feeling the speed build up, hearing the whisper of air brushing past the canopy turn to a moan, then a scream, then rise to a faint whistle, now as familiar to my ear as the night peeping of treetoads back in New Hampshire. That persistent sound in nature simply meant sleep to me as a small boy. This sound meant flight.

Heming's wheels lifted off and started retracting. I felt I must be off too, though the plane was mushy. Groping with my left hand for the landing gear toggle switch, I snapped it up. And at that moment, while the act of flight was still breathlessly tentative, Heming's plane banked inexorably toward me and began its turn.

You have to understand that an Airacobra was a very skittish little beast that got off the ground only reluctantly and sought every excuse to return to it, violently or not. Any plane that's barely flying should be kept straight and level for that moment of transition. It needs all the lift it can get, just then, and shouldn't be discouraged from flight by banking for a turn. Banking diminishes lift.

To a P-39, such a turn right at that fragile moment of takeoff was an outrage. If an element leader made such a turn, right toward a wingman, perhaps 10 feet away, who wasn't yet properly in the air, guys on the ground would certainly call to their friends to come and watch the crash.

I felt I couldn't turn without stalling out. Barely moving my soft controls, I managed to squeeze under Heming, clawing for air while the wheels slowly came up. Then, with speed building, I slid into position on Heming's left wing instead of his right. He looked around at me angrily.

We flew the same mission to Wau. Up through the pass, orbiting while the transports lumbered onto the hillside strip, one by one, and then roared off again. I switched tanks at the right time. I searched the sky faithfully. Nothing happened. At last we came out of the mountains, ripped low over the jungle, stormed over Moresby at treetop level, buzzed the strip, peeled up and away into the traffic pattern, dropped wheels and flaps, and skimmed onto the steel matting. Heming was waiting for me outside the alert shack.

"What the hell's the matter with you? Don't you know how to fly?"

"Not well enough to make that turn on takeoff," I said. "I didn't have flying speed."

"Of course you had flying speed. I had flying speed, and you were right with me."

"I was barely off the ground when you turned into me, for God's sake."

"Next time you fly my wing, you make that fucking turn with me."

"I will as soon as I learn how to do it," I said. "If I don't have flying speed, you make that fucking turn alone, and I'll catch you later."

He stared at me, and for a moment I thought he was going to smile. Then he walked off to get some coffee. I stretched out on a cot and gazed up at the thatched roof. If that turn on takeoff was part of knowing how to fly a fighter, then Heming was right. I was hopeless. I also realized, with some bemusement, that I really didn't give a damn.

This kind of flying was Heming's entire career. He'd learned it during long months of peacetime boredom. He'd become a true "hot pilot," in the prewar army tradition of Eddie Rickenbacker, Jimmy Doolittle, Claire Chennault, Charles Lindbergh, Hap Arnold, Tooey Spaatz, all of those and more.

In contrast, I was what we called a GI pilot, a civilian taking time off to do a strange, dangerous job for reasons that started by being patriotic and maybe got a little out of hand. My ambition was not to be a bemedaled ace, but to do my small best and somehow, eventually, get out of there. My aim in life, you might say, was to hang on to it.

It was only a couple of days later that I had breakfast with Willy Meecham, one of the replacements whose tent adjoined ours. I hadn't known him very well—hadn't realized that he'd been married only seven days when we were all scraped up from our various operational training units and sent to California to board our Norwegian freighter.

"Missing her is awful," he said. "She's so damn far away. This place is so...*final*. I guess I'd like it better here if it wasn't for her."

"What are you going to do after the war?" I asked, changing the subject.

"I want to set up a sort of camp for rich people back in Colorado. You know, hunting, fishing, skiing, mountain climbing. I'd fly 'em in and out, and we'd have nice cabins or something where they'd stay, and we'd cook up great food for them, and have a long bar with a mirror behind it."

"And you'd charge them plenty."

"You bet."

"Sounds good," I said. "How about a job?"

"You're hired. But first I've got to fly Heming's wing on the second escort. We're going to Wau twice today, eight planes a mission. Got to get down there."

He ducked out, squirming into his shoulder holster as he left. I heard a jeep rattle off.

Twenty minutes later Willy Meecham was dead. The report was that he'd caught a wing on takeoff and cartwheeled, and of course the plane had blown up. All that fuel.

I knew exactly what had happened. Heming had made his hot-pilot turn the moment his wheels started retracting—right into his wingman. I guess he wanted to see how good a pilot he'd drawn this time. Meecham had tried to do the right thing—to turn with him. I hadn't had the guts to do that. So I was still alive.

No one said anything about Meecham. I guess there wasn't enough of him left for a funeral.

A few days later, coming back from Wau, we got a call from the sector there, loud and clear and very demanding in our earphones: "Beaver, Beaver, we have bandits, we have bandits."

Adrenalin surged through me like a shot of whiskey. I scoured the sky, looking for those strange planes that I had never seen, fast and dangerous and bright with their scarlet circles. There was nothing, just our drab little Airacobras, and below us the dingy, weather-stained transports.

Herkimer, who was leading us that day, called the Wau codeword and then: "Beaver cannot be with you. No can do. Do you read me? No can do."

We had just left the pass, and it seemed possible to turn back and tangle with them, but we wouldn't have had fuel to get home. Back on the ground, we talked about it. Some of the pilots swore and groaned about missing a chance for combat. They said they would have bounced the enemy and ripped them apart and then gone on home with the mixture leaned out. They'd have made it all right, they said.

"No, you wouldn't," Herkimer said, mildly. "Combat means full throttle. You couldn't have gotten home."

On the whole, I was relieved to have combat postponed. I was pretty sure I wasn't good enough yet to go blazing around the sky with flaming guns while a bunch of dedicated Japanese dove expertly upon me from out of the sun.

We heard exactly the same message from Wau the next day when we were at exactly the same place—the point of no return. Obviously, enemy spotters knew our range to the mile, and just when to call in the Lilys and Sallys to bomb the heaped-up supplies and disorganized replacements at the Wau strip. I had a feeling that the war was coming closer every day.

"I wish we'd get into it," Steve said. We were in our sacks in the quiet tent, both wanting to sleep because we were both posted for the next day.

"Do you feel ready for it?" I asked. "I don't."

"But that doesn't matter," Steve said. "We just have to do it, ready or not."

"Yeah, but the longer it takes, the better I feel."

Ben Briker came in with his flashlight. He wasn't posted, so he'd been pounding down a few drinks at the Farmhouse. "You guys got to get some sack," he said. "You got to go flying in about twenty minutes." That was a squadron saying. If you were on early call you were always reminded that you only had "about twenty minutes" to sleep.

"What about you, Ben?" said Steve. "Don't you want to hit the Japs and get it over with?"

"Yeah, I guess so," Ben said, absently.

"I don't," I said. "I want a few more days."

"Yeah, that sounds good too. I've got tomorrow."

"Hell, Ben," said Steve. "You're hopeless."

Uncertainly, I finally drifted off to sleep.

C H A P T E R
S I X

SCRAMBLING

Next morning, our Wau escort was canceled, and we were kept on ground alert. We sat in the shack interminably, waiting for the operations phone to ring. The cards riffled and people murmured quietly over the endless Monopoly game, and "San Antonio Rose" emerged scratchily from the wind-up Victrola at least eight times—whenever someone remembered to crank the thing. "San Antonio Rose" was our only record.

We'd developed a new fad—shaving our forearms. Everyone seemed to have a sheath knife of some kind, and most people wore them on the inside of the shin, where you could get at them in a hurry to cut a strap or a line or the parachute shrouds. I'd brought along a hunting knife I'd had since I was 15. It was in a leather sheath, shiny and dark with long use, and I had stitched the sheath into permanent position beside the map pocket of my flying suit, which was on the right shin. When I put on the flying suit, I put on the knife too.

Somehow we got competitive about how sharp our knives were. Old pilots who had been on leave to Sydney came back with little whetstones along with the usual cheeses, salamis, and big brown bottles of beer. And then they'd hone their knives endlessly, with growing skill, even artistry. And they'd test them by shaving patches of hair off their forearms. All the old pilots had bare patches on their arms. We replacements could barely wait to go on leave so we could get whetstones and shave our arms too.

Waiting there that day, you could hear, between quiet Monopoly arguments and playings of "San Antonio Rose," the sibilant sound of good steel being whetted and then the faint rasp of razor-sharp blades scything hair. Then the phone rang.

It had happened twice before, and everything had gone dead still while the operations clerk plucked the phone from its leather box and said "Fohty-first Fahter" in his Louisiana accent. And then he'd said something like "Oh, hi, Pete, how y'all doin' over theah?" and we'd gone back to shuffling and turning pages and murmuring and sharpening.

This time the lad said "Fohty-first Fahter," and then was quiet for a moment, and then said "Right," and hung up.

"Scramble two flights!" he called out. "Angels Twenty! Dog Six and Vector Ninety."

Two flights was all we had on alert. "Angels" meant thousands of feet. "Dog Six" was a coordinate on the little grid map each of us carried in that pocket where I'd sown my knife. "Vector Ninety" meant that once we got to that coordinate—just north of Moresby—we'd fly east (90 degrees). That would take us over the Kakoda Trail and across the Owen Stanleys toward Dobodura.

I was thinking about all that as I zipped up my flying suit, slid into my holster straps, and ran to a jeep that was just moving. I flung myself on it and clung while we bounded out to the flight line. I leapt off at my revetment and ran to the plane. The crew chief was on the wing, reaching down for me with one hand, holding my Mae West with the other.

He yanked me up beside him and quickly slapped the orange life preserver around my neck, clicking the straps as I entered the cockpit door. Then he held the parachute straps open so I could get my arms in when I sat down. Helmet and goggles were over the stick. I had them on in a second. Oxygen mask went over my head, and the crew chief clicked the tube into the oxygen lead while I tightened my throat microphone.

Before I knew it, my parachute straps were fastened and the Sutton harness was in place with a click. The man gripped my shoulder and pointed at the energizer. As I shoved it down with my heel, he yelled "Good luck!" gave me a little pat, and jumped off the wing.

The whine built up as I snapped on the fuel pump and cracked the throttle. Then I rolled the toe of my boot down to engage the engine, and pumped twice on the primer as the prop wheeled in front of me. With a gasp and a bark the Allison came alive, and I trundled out of the revetment, waving thanks to the crew chief. Everyone was rolling, but by luck, I came up beside John G.'s plane. He was Red Leader and I was Number Four that day, last man in the flight. It was said to be the spot for the most expendable pilot.

I didn't think of that. I didn't think of going into combat. I didn't think of anything except getting this crate off the ground without doing something stupid. That's what a scramble was all about—getting off the ground before the pilot had time to think.

No magneto check, no engine run-up. We taxied fast to the strip and took off in pairs, pretty much the way we were supposed to. John G. went with Horachov on his wing. Canuck and I formed the second element. We got into position, and Canuck waggled his ailerons—my cue to pour on the coal—and then just as his plane began to roll he crossed himself. Jesus Christ, I thought, this must be serious business.

We started our takeoff run before the first element was off the ground. Then they began their turn—not Heming's turn, but a wide, gentle swing, the planes going fast. Canuck and I were able to turn easily inside them and so put the flight in proper formation. By the time we were on course for the coordinate, Blue Flight was with us, all in position except that Foxey Shriver, who was supposed to be Number Two, had ended up Number Four—"tail-ass Charlie" for our two flights.

Would he be OK? I wondered, as we started to climb. For that matter, would I be OK? I swiveled my head, searching for whatever it was that had sent us scrambling. My eyes got tired with staring around and peeking as close to the sun as I could. I was frantically aware that my life depended on seeing something.

None of us saw anything. We reached 20,000 feet, and flew over Dobodura, and stooged around, dodging the buildup of clouds, and there wasn't another plane in the sky. Just our two flights. Sector called us and gave us an "all clear," so we headed back to Moresby, all nice and relaxed. It had been just a peacetime outing. Japanese? Forget it. There weren't any.

With the excitement of that first scramble over, we got back to the routine "milk runs" to Wau, which had become boring even to us new pilots. For the rest of March 1943 and into April, we escorted the C-47s every day, sometimes twice a day. I felt I could fly that route in my sleep. I knew the course instinctively, and the landscape was getting familiar. I recognized many of the jagged peaks, generally hidden in cloud, but sometimes appearing, like the fangs of a striking snake, shockingly near our altitude.

I knew various valleys by their shade of green, the size of their streams, the amount of mist that gathered in them. I knew "Bulldog," the primitive airstrip that had been hacked into a mountainside south of Wau. Looking down on it from a fighter, it seemed too tiny for any airplane. But we knew it would work for small planes in an emergency. Even a P-39 could belly in there—a friend in another squadron did that, and got himself safely back to base.

I knew Wau, of course. I can still see it as it was from 10,000 feet: the airstrip a brown scar on the green hillside, the gleam of a few shacks with corrugated steel roofs, the spray of litter against the jungle growth, sometimes the faint haze of gunfire, hanging low on the earth. I also knew the weather and instinctively checked for the first strands of mist, sure signal that we must dash to safety, southward, away from the mountains' boiling cumulus—more deadly to us than the Japanese.

Only a handful of our planes had decent flight instruments—artificial horizon and gyro compass—and they were presumably flown by flight leaders. Many other planes had holes in their dashboards where instruments had been yanked out to save weight. If a flight got into the murk, the procedure was for its leader to go on instruments and the other three to stick to him like leeches. Actually, only three or four of the old-time flight leaders, like Heming, could fly competently on instruments, anyway. The rest of us GI pilots weren't fully trained for blind or night flying.

In April, we felt that something different was going to happen. No one said anything, but pilots who weren't scheduled for the escort to Wau began to be kept on ground alert. The rumor was that the Australian coast watchers were calling in lots of enemy activity at Lae, on the north coast. We might have to scramble again. OK. I could do that. I knew how to dash out to the plane, whip it off the ground without checking a damn thing, stagger up to 20,000 feet, glare around at the sky, and orbit back down to a landing. Nothing to it.

I was off-duty the day the squadron was scrambled down toward Milne Bay. They didn't see anything, but this time they heard the excited voices of pilots from another fighter group calling in bandits and shouting warnings. Steve flew that mission and said it was maddening, because the voices sounded so near, yet the sky around Beaver squadron was empty. "Somebody was having a real soiree," he said. That was the squadron word for a fight. We used it whenever we could.

Next morning the whole squadron was on alert. Yesterday's scramble had been a real one, not just a chase after a thunderstorm or a flock of birds. The Japanese had raided Milne Bay, and some P-40 squadrons, both American and RAAF, had tangled with them. The feeling was that the enemy would try again at Milne Bay or somewhere else, maybe even Moresby. Even Jeff, the C.O., and Guthrie, the operations officer, were ready to scramble with us. They'd be "Beaver Green." We were very quiet, and I had to hurry to the latrine a couple of times.

At about ten in the morning the phone rang. Everyone shut up and stared at the operations clerk as he answered: "Fohty-first Fahter"…"Got it"…Click.

"Scramble all flights!" he shouted. "Angels Twenty-three over the area!"

A coffee cup clanged as someone threw it toward the smoko truck. I was zipped up and into my shoulder holster in a flash. The last thing I heard as I jumped at a moving jeep and clung was "San Antonio Rose" running down on the Victrola: "My Rose, m-y-y R-o-s-e of Sa-a-a-n A-a-a-n-n-n- …." Painful. No one was rewinding.

I jumped off at a revetment and sprang for the wing of Number 75. The crew chief hauled me up: Mae West over my head and hooked, left leg into the cockpit, over the short control stick, then right. Parachute straps snapping tight around the thighs and over the chest while I slipped on helmet with oxygen mask attached. Leads for oxygen, earphones, and mike clicking and radio coming alive in my ears as I turned on switches and clamped my heel on the energizer. Shoulder harness meeting safety belt at the broad leather patch where one buckle secured the whole thing. Crew chief's hand gripping my shoulder before he jumped clear and I rolled my foot forward to engage.

Wheeling prop. Rippling thunder from below and behind. Brakes off and wheels rolling. There was Number 70—John G.'s plane. I was to fly his wing if we scrambled. Well, we were doing it, and I was in position. A nod from him. Ailerons waving their signal. Throttle forward...smoothly...all...the...*way*....And we were off. Off to see the Wizard.

I remember climbing as steeply as we could, looking around, seeing nothing except our own four flights. We seemed to gain altitude more quickly than before. I guess we had the throttles wide open, gulping fuel. After all, there was no need to save it—we were right over our own strip.

We orbited as we climbed. Abruptly, tall columns of dark-brown smoke rose from Moresby, far below us. Bombs were obviously falling, hitting an oil depot, from the look of it. My earphones had been busy with mumbled directions from the Moresby sector to the fighter squadrons that were all scrambling. Now a calm voice—must have been from an old pilot—said, "Beaver, two o'clock level." Instantly, I was looking at a cluster of black specks against the clouds. They appeared out of nowhere, as though a giant vandal had flicked a brush, wet with ink, toward a landscape painting.

How could anyone tell these dark blobs were the Japanese? Were we about to take part in just another military gaffe—blasting away at a bunch of Australian Beauforts or something? If these were Japanese, they looked too big for fighters. Where were the Zeroes?

We moved toward them on a converging course, still trying to climb, to wrench more sky under our poor, mismatched

'39s. I spun my head frantically in every direction, searching for the bright, elegant fighters with red circles that I had pictured. Not a one. When I glanced back at our target, I found we had inched closer, and clawed about 1000 feet higher than the specks—which had grown into planes, big, husky dark-colored bombers with high tails. They looked exactly like our B-26s. That was it! We were about to cut loose on our own medium bombers. Oops! Sorry! Hey, those things happen, right?

Suddenly something terrible happened to John G.'s plane, right beside me. A great piece of its bottom fell off and tumbled away. Belly tank! My God, we were really going in.

I switched tanks, found the belly-tank release handle, which I'd never touched before, and gave it a healthy yank. The plane suddenly felt light as a feather, wondrously agile and responsive. I would have loved to have flown it for a little while, to enjoy it, but John G. was dropping his nose toward that formation, now close enough to see the gleaming plexiglass and a dark-green color and—*yes*—darkish red circles with a thin white rim. Japanese Betty bombers.

I snapped on my gunsight and gun switches, and watched the planes get a little bigger in the circle of light on my armor glass. I was breathing very fast, and moving very quickly, and I jumped against my straps when another plane appeared ahead of us, diving straight down at the bombers, trailing brown smoke.

A P-38. Unmistakable twin booms. Must have been hit up above us. All that smoke.

As I thought that, the smoke abruptly stopped. Then John G.'s plane began to do the same thing—stream brownish smoke—and I realized it came from his guns. I'd never seen gunsmoke from all the guns firing.

Now I watched the nearest Betty get a little closer, and since my leader was firing, I did too. There was a wonderful hammering sound and the cockpit filled with smoke. My eyes hurt and watered, and I had trouble seeing the target. Then John G. flicked away to the left, and of course I followed. We climbed away together and turned back for another pass.

I didn't like this at all. Not because of my upbringing in a serenely pacifist family, not because of the education that had instilled in me the tenet that war was the ultimate insanity. I didn't like my first baptism of battle because I felt we had broken away too soon and hadn't scored enough hits.

We bored in the second time, and when the fumes streamed from John G.'s plane I held off, waiting to get a little closer. The bomber in my gunsight was larger than before, and the port engine was trailing a dark smudge of smoke. It was falling behind the other Bettys. I let it fill the sight and overlap a bit, and then I held the trigger down and squinted my eyes against the damn smoke.

John G. broke away, but I stayed just a tad longer. I saw flashes along the Betty's fuselage—surely they must be mine. I shot for another half-second (it seemed like five seconds), and then whipped away in a nice chandelle to latch onto my leader again. It was a beautiful chandelle, right out of flying school, ball centered, needle pointing the turn, the plane solidly under my buttocks the way it is in a perfectly coordinated maneuver.

And at the top of it, a totally new sound shocked me—a rattle like hail on a tin roof. What the hell was that? I wondered. Had something come loose?

I glanced out at my wings and something about them disturbed me. I looked carefully and saw that on both upper-wing surfaces—especially the right—the aluminum seemed torn. It appeared to have sprouted little jagged rings of metal.

Bullet holes! Some bastard had shot at me!

I screwed my head around and found no planes behind me. I searched for John G. and couldn't find him. But the Betty was still on its course to the north, lagging far behind. Apparently that son of a bitch had shot back at me. He'd tried to kill me, for God's sake!

I started after the big bomber with blood in my eye. If they wanted to play rough....

Then I glanced again at my wings. They looked diseased. I wondered what else was hit, and nervously scanned my engine instruments: tachometer, oil pressure, oil temperature, that sort of stuff. All the needles were in the green. The plane seemed to fly well, but I realized I was a little high-strung just then. Perhaps my judgment was askew. Those wings looked pretty bad.

And so a calming injection of good, old-fashioned fear stilled my anger and probably saved my life. It also, I'm sure, kept me off the roll of heroes, for I know I'd have clobbered that Betty had I made another pass. I'd gotten the idea of it. I could picture what I would do, how my shots would look getting inside that big, tubular fuselage. A flyer, like an athlete, must hold an image of his actions in his head in order to carry them out correctly. I had a clear filmstrip running through my brain: nosing down on the Betty; turning in; aiming ahead of the nose—not so far, just *there*—and firing.

I saw it vividly. I still see it sometimes at 3:45 in the morning when my old man's plumbing wakes me. I know I'd have gotten him. Then the correspondents would have picked it up, and maybe I'd have made *Life* magazine: "Plane Riddled, New Guinea Pilot Downs Jap Bomber—and Dies." Hell of a story!

Perhaps I should have done it. But that burst of recklessness gave way to cowardice, and I cut back my throttle and dropped the nose toward the tall feathers of smoke still rising from Moresby's oil depot. I slid down to my strip, spotted the landing T which indicated the pattern direction, and without the usual low-level fly-past, turned onto base leg, wheels and flaps down.

I greased it on, slowed my landing run, opened the windows to get some fresh air, and noticed a fire truck on my wing. I turned off the strip toward my revetment, and found an ambulance now joining the procession. I wondered if the 41st always did this when its Beavers returned from a soiree.

The crew chief jumped on my left wing before I'd braked to a stop. "Don't light a cigarette, for Christ sake!" he shouted. I cut the engine, undid my sweat-soaked straps, and clambered out on the wing. My knees were shaking, uncontrollably.

The crew chief helped me down. "You OK, lieutenant?"

"Fine," I said.

He gestured silently at a brooklet of raw gasoline dribbling from below the wing and forming a glittering pond in the dirt. He also pointed wordlessly to my left main wheel. The tire was flat. So was the nose wheel tire. "They got you real good," he said.

Indeed they had. Some 140 bullet holes were counted in that poor old crate before the assessment was canceled and the plane junked. A 20-millimeter cannon shell had exploded on the engine block without stopping that Allison. Two 7.7-millimeter bullets had passed within a foot of my skinny—but warm—body. The direction of the bullets indicated that I'd been hit by two of the Betty's guns as I made that chandelle I had been so proud of.

I thought John G. would chew me out for leaving him. He didn't. "We were all screwed up, anyway," he said, "and the Zeroes were tangling with the '38s, not us. I just though you'd gotten shot down."

"Zeroes?" I said.

"You didn't see 'em? Hell, man, the sky was full of 'em, up above the Bettys."

Jeff, the C.O., bought me a drink that night. "Between us all we got that bomber," he said, "so they won't be able to score you as a 'probable.' That ought to cheer you up."

"I got some hits on it," I said, wondering for the first time if I could make a claim on part of a plane.

"Yeah, we all did," he said, absently.

That was the last big daylight raid on Moresby—April 12, 1943. The enemy sent up more than 100 planes and lost a bunch. The P-38s had a field day—they always did. The P-40s also got some, but lost some too. The Beavers claimed two planes, but lost four. Keating and Ferguson had been seen to bail out. But John E., a good old veteran, simply vanished in the mountains, the deep valleys, the mat of jungle, or the endless swamps. The fourth plane lost was mine.

I got a day off the next day, then was posted on Heming's wing. We went out to our revetments together, and he said nothing about staying with him on takeoff. What he said was, "Next time, skid your turns. They can't hit you if you skid." Then he went to his plane.

My dose of real combat changed my life considerably. I was gratified at having gotten through a rite of passage, yet disturbed at not having done better. I had no blood lust, no aching desire to kill, but a pilot gets used to thinking of his job as a matter of compulsory excellence—"if ya wanna keep livin', ya gotta fly right"—and picking up 140-odd bullet holes indicated that I'd flown wrong.

Clearly, I was a long shot in the race to survive. In my head I could hear the voices of the Beavers, chattering away at the Farmhouse bar on an evening not too far in the future:

"Hey, Park finally bought it, huh? Jeez, that's tough. I kinda liked him."

"Yeah. He wasn't a bad pilot, either. He just...you know...didn't quite have it."

The vision was all too logical. But I rebelled at it, sometimes with the confidence instilled by a couple of shots of whiskey (Didn't have it, eh? I'd show 'em!), sometimes with intricate schemes for avoiding danger devised in the black of night when I awoke nervously just before the charge-of-quarters' watchman's rattle and his shout: "Early flights! Early flights!"

I had one strange and unlikely thing going for me: To my own astonishment, I'd honestly enjoyed combat. I had loved the feel of the plane, the reckless sweep into position, the target in the sight, the hammer and thump of the machine guns and the cannon between my legs, the red curve of the tracers reaching out. I *knew* I could do it again, much better. I could picture skidding when I broke away, just as Heming had said. That would work. I could feel it. So there I was, scared but eager, anxious to have another chance, yet dreading it.

Ferguson had returned to the squadron soon after bailing out during the April 12 soiree. He'd been over the area and had no trouble. But Dick Keating had vanished. One of the Zeroes that I never saw had clobbered him and lots of people had seen him hit the silk. It hadn't seemed very far from Moresby, but it was tough country, the foothills of the Stanleys.

The days passed without Keating, and gradually we wrote him out of our minds. Stories went around about men who had bailed out in sight of their own home strips and had never again been seen. The great swamps of New Guinea, some stretching right to the edge of the Moresby area, had simply swallowed them. If people had vanished forever only minutes away from making a landing, what chance had Keating? I hadn't known him very well, but remembered a handsome, athletic young man, quick and bright and fun to talk to. Steve had known him better than I, and felt his loss.

We were both on duty in the alert shack, back from the morning milk run to Wau, when a jeep swirled to a stop outside and above the rattle of the engine we heard an Australian voice: "So long, mate. Good luck to you," and an American voice: "Thanks again for everything," and in walked Keating, carrying his escape kit, which formed the detachable back pad of our parachutes. He was wearing clean khakis. He had recently shaved. But the thing we noticed most was a different look about his face. Instead of being haggard and lined, it was filled out, younger-looking.

We all fell upon him gladly and pummeled him and called him an old bastard and asked him a thousand questions at once. Finally we shut up to let him talk.

A Zero had gotten a burst into him, and after diving away, he'd found the plane streaming smoke (since the engine was mounted behind the cockpit, he didn't see it until he craned around for a look; but he smelled it). He'd aimed back toward Moresby, but when he had to leave the plane he was still miles away.

With the heat increasing and still 3000 feet under him, Keating had shucked off his door and rolled out. "I see now why we keep the leg straps tight," he told us. "The 'chute opens so suddenly that I swear those straps would snap your balls off if they were loose."

He'd floated down into scrubby growth on a hillside, rolled up his parachute, sat back to have a cigarette and get his mind working properly, the way we'd all been told to do, and almost immediately found some Papuans staring at him. By luck, he'd come down near a native garden, and a whole village had watched him.

Keating had never learned any of Carl Jacobsen's Pidgin English, but the natives had a few English words, and by smiles and gestures he got through to them that he was friendly, and wanted to get back to Moresby. They took him to their village. They didn't let him walk. "They carried me on a sort of litter rigged out of poles," he told us. "I didn't need to be carried, but they did it. It was fine."

So he spent 10 days, this healthy young man, lolling on his litter like Cleopatra as he was passed from village to village on the way to the end of a track big enough for a jeep. At every village he was given fresh roast pork to eat. It was always ready, though he never figured out how the people learned that he was coming.

"I never had it so good," he said. "Hell, I could smell the roast pork two miles away, day after day. Marvelous! I gained twelve pounds!" No wonder he looked different.

The U.S. Army, in its wisdom, deemed Keating badly in need of leave after his terrible ordeal, so on top of his two weeks' rest cure with the natives, he got sent to Sydney to eat steak and eggs and drink himself silly. When Jeff told him the news, he just shook his head. "When I get back," he said. "let's have another soiree. I want to get shot down again."

Keating had been picked up at the jeep track by a patrol from ANGAU. The acronym stood for Australia–New Guinea Administrative Unit. Their people supervised the natives, holding them together, keeping them employed by the troops, trying to keep the American Fifth Air Force from overpaying them.

We learned all this from the Australian liaison officer assigned to our 35th Fighter Group. Amstead was an artillery captain, rather slightly built for an Australian, who managed to remain every inch a soldier yet unbend delightfully when he joined us in our alert shack or around the Farmhouse bar. It was he who gently pointed out how the Yanks were wrecking New Guinea's economy. The "Boongs" (as we soon learned to call them in those racist days) had willingly worked for something like a cigarette a day until we Americans began giving them real wages.

"You Yanks get too much bloody pay," said Amstead. "You're destroying the way things work."

We'd never thought of that, and it made sense. The Australian troops—the "Diggers"—had some system of withholding part of their military pay so they'd have something to come home to. That seemed like a good idea, but of course we Americans didn't do it. So we could always outspend our allies, and earn their resentment, in the good old American way.

It was funny how many things we started to question as we spent day after day, through April and May of 1943, flying endlessly to Wau with the transports in planes that were never built for escort work, that couldn't get enough altitude to compete with the enemy. There was the matter of our personal equipment. The RAAF had beautiful fleece-lined flying boots, for example. We just had GI boots, the same as what a dogface in the infantry wore. They were OK for us on the ground when worn without socks, since we didn't walk much, but they were cold in the air. A P-39 was apt to get a cold blast coming up around the stick where its protective rubber sleeve had rotted away in the jungle climate. Struggling up to 20,000 feet could be cold work. We craved those Aussie boots.

We also coveted the Smith & Wesson revolver that the Aussie pilots carried. It was a .38 and you could hit things with it—a bird, maybe, or a wild pig, or a wallaby—something remotely edible when you were shot down in the jungle and needed food. We had the old .45 Colt automatic—heavy, awkward, untrustworthy, and accurate only when you threw it at your target.

, We badly wanted to arrange some sort of trade, and for once we Americans ran into a piece of luck: The Aussies, it turned out, were ogling our old Colts even more avidly than we were leering at their Smith & Wessons. They probably knew of some place on the mainland where they could sell them for a fortune.

We learned that with a little finagling, and perhaps a few long-out-of-date copies of *Time* or *Saturday Evening Post* thrown in, we could get *both* the boots and the revolver for a hastily cleaned and derusted Colt with as much ammunition as we could cadge. The deal made a lot of people happy.

I didn't go for it. Someone told me that when you bailed out with flying boots on they were apt to slide right off your feet when the 'chute opened. Since I felt I had every probability of bailing out and trudging a couple of hundred miles, I decided to continue flying in my GI boots. I would have liked the revolver, but as a cadet I'd scored "Expert" with a Colt, and it had become comfortable to carry, sitting there, rusting away under my armpit. I had nothing in my escape kit that would provide meat for dinner if and when I was down in the jungle. I handled that problem by trying not to think about it.

I did eventually take up cudgels, though, to adopt the British system for transmitting on the radio. Our obsolete throat mikes turned every word into a garbled squawk unless you pinched the device against your larynx. But since the transmitter button was on the throttle handle, you had to let go of the stick in order to squeeze the mike with your right hand while you pushed the button with your left.

In an Airacobra, this was insane. The little beast would fall out of the sky if you didn't keep it there with your right hand—and you seldom had to touch your throttle with your left. So why wasn't the mike button on the stick where it belonged? Answer: That was the RAF way of doing it, not the American. It took about a year before the change was adopted.

We began to learn a bit about Moresby. The Aussies had an officers' club overlooking the harbor, and Jeff said we were welcomed there, so we used to put on clean khaki pants and take a jeep into town. The Australians weren't exactly over-joyed. They had real old army traditions of behaving decorous-ly at officers' mess—all that stuff—and we were a bit noisy as fighter pilots are when they come out from under the tension. And our clothes were sloppy-looking, and most of us forgot to wear our rank.

The food wasn't great, but it was eight times better than our "boeuf de boullie," as Kelvin called it. Sometimes as we left in the evening and piled into a couple of jeeps to drive back to the squadron, we'd listen to the Papuans sing, outside, by the harbor. They had a great knack for harmony, and they'd sing mission hymns and their own chants with these fine deep chords, and we'd listen quietly for a bit and then rattle back to our home, singing our own songs.

Singing was pretty big in our squadron because some of the pilots had trained in Canada and picked up RAF songs. Everyone knew "I've Got Sixpence" and "Bless 'Em All," but there were others, fine tuneful songs so dirty I can't even write the titles. We had our own American songs too, like "There Once Was an Indian Maid," "O'Riley's Daughter," and others that people had made up along the way:

> *A young fighter pilot to Sydney did crawl*
>
> *He'd just come back from a raid on Rabaul,*
>
> *When an old MP sergeant said "Pardon me, please.*
>
> *You've blood on your tunic and mud on your knees."*

That one told a whole long story. We had others that moaned about being too young to die and just wanting to go home:

> *These P-39s how they rattle and roar,*
>
> *I don't want to fly over Buna no more!*

And some that took cracks at the staff people down on the mainland, the people that were paid per diem—"p.d. boys," we called them, or "paddle feet."

> *I wish I was in old Brisbane*
>
> *To hear those p.d. boys complain:*
>
> > *It's hardships, hardships.*
> >
> > *You don't know what hardships are!*

> *Six bucks a day plus regular pay*
>
> *And the Nips two thousand miles away!*
>
> > *It's hardships, you bastards.*
> >
> > *You don't know what hardships are!*

Every so often the flight surgeon, McDermott ("Doctor Mac") would indicate to Jeff that it was time for a balloon. That meant he'd mix up hospital alcohol with ground-up fruit drops that the Red Cross had once dumped on us, and dilute it so it would go around, and all the pilots who weren't flying the next day—plus a few old-timers who got drunk every night anyway, whether they flew next day or not—would get smashed and bellow the songs in what we considered glorious harmony, and roll off to bed, often chucking up on the way. It was pretty awful, but it broke the endless routine. And the singing was great.

Sometimes two or three of us would take a jeep and explore the coast for a way. We'd come to native settlements with decorated long houses, and houses up on stilts, and women and children staring at us, not sure whether or not to be afraid. The women were bare-breasted, but their skin was often wretchedly scaly or moldy-looking. So when we returned to the squadron and told them where we'd been, and they all chorused the usual squadron question: "Did you get any?" it was really a pretty gross idea.

I never heard of anyone getting any in such places, but I imagine it happened, because it was a big war with lots of different kinds of people. We had a few nurses in Moresby, and Ferguson, who considered himself dangerously oversexed, swore that he'd worked out an arrangement with a flashy blonde from Pittsburg whom we'd all whistled at from afar. Ferg said he was "gettin' it regular," but you couldn't really take his word for it.

We were scrambled a few other times, but with no solid target to go after. And we were bombed rather desultorily by an occasional night raider—probably a Dinah. The red alert was supposed to be three shots from an ack-ack gun, but usually the shots were for real, aimed at the target.

One antiaircraft unit moved right next to our squadron, and we groaned a little about it, thinking of the noise of those guns going off at close range. Then I saw a familiar face over in their area, and found a university classmate, now a lieutenant in this Connecticut National Guard battery. We hadn't known each other that well, but now we clutched at each other affectionately and I had chow with him—their food was better than ours—and showed him our planes.

It occurred to me that Jack's specialty was to shoot down aircraft, and mine was—among other things—to avoid being shot down by flak, so we arranged a little reciprocating information. All our off-duty pilots gathered at the battery to see how the guns worked and to brief the gunners on how we jinked and skidded to throw them off. I remember those great 90-millimeter guns going off, just for us: a heavy bang followed by a sort of humming sound, echoing, fading quickly. And as we looked up we'd see a far-distant blossom of smoke with a bright spot in the center, then some seconds later hear a faint "pop."

"It doesn't seem like much," we said to the gunners.

"Just keep dodging," they said.

The 35th Group had a rescue boat in the harbor, and sometimes some of us would take it out and do a little fishing or exploring along the shore. A couple of days after I'd barely survived the great Japanese air raid, I joined a fishing trip, and someone hooked something very logy, half afloat, and drew it to the gunwale. It was a flying suit, much like our own, but with wires running through it to heat it electrically. It had Japanese writing on it, and we thought we had a great prize for the group intelligence officer. We started to pull it in, then suddenly let it go overboard. There was part of a man's body in it.

CHAPTER SEVEN

ISLANDS IN A SEA OF BOREDOM

The old adage of war being nine-tenths boredom and one-tenth panic was fully borne out for me in May and June of 1943. As flying weather improved—as it seems to do in New Guinea at that time of the year—we flew sometimes twice a day to Wau, and I became as accustomed to it as a cat to the barn. As my flight hours increased, so did my competence, and also a certain wary confidence.

As I look back now, only a few scenes emerge from the gray sameness of those days. There was the arrival of more replacements and the sudden realization that I was now one of the "old guys." Ironically, these replacements had picked up a lot of time in the Seventh Air Force at Panama, and were really more experienced on P-39s than I, but at least I knew my way around Papua.

Finally, I began to be posted occasionally as Number Three in the flight—element leader. Now I could take the left lane at takeoff, checking to my right to see that Number Four was in position, waggling my ailerons at him when it was time to go, even reminding him, over breakfast coffee, to keep his head turning, his eyes moving and searching.

"How did Fisher make out?" John G. asked me after a mission with two replacements on our wings.

"Good pilot, but he stared at me too much. He hasn't learned to see anything yet." I felt very important.

"Takes a while," said John G.

We had a couple of scrambles interspersed with all those escort missions, but nothing happened. Thundershowers, probably. That early radar bounced off thunderstorms as though they were squadrons of Bettys coming in on a bombing run.

There was the north coast interlude. Two flights spent a few days flying out of Dobodura. No ground crews, just eight of us Beavers sharing tents and chow with a P-40 squadron, preflighting our own planes every morning, then flying patrols up to Salamaua and back.

It was good to be cut free of the squadron for a little, to act on our own without the strictures—however loose and informal—of the squadron hierarchy. It was fun to "join" another outfit for a while, especially since we knew many of the people. Fifth Fighter Command was like a small town, back then. We had only a few fighter groups, and all the pilots pretty much knew one another.

I felt sorry when our four or five days at Dobodura ended. Yet we were all glad to be heading back to our own tents, our own chow (the chow we'd been sharing was just as awful as ours), our own whiskey, our own "San Antonio Rose" on the Victrola.

We flew back to Moresby through a little square-cut pass in the ridge of the Owen Stanleys which we called the Gunsight, because that's how it looked. We approached it from the north, where it was high country, reaching up closer and closer to our planes. Then we slammed through the pass, going like a salvo of bullets, two flights of four, all tucked in tight, wingtips overlapping so we'd fit between those high, squared-off rock walls.

As we shot through to the south side, we all dropped together momentarily, for here the mountains simply ended in a sheer cliff. The ground seemed to vanish under us, and we pointed our sharp little noses at the distant blue curve of Port Moresby and howled downhill above the rain forest and the glimmering swamps of the coastal plain. It was the air, streaming through the Gunsight from north to south, that sank as it rushed over that mighty cliff and gave our two flights their strange little hiccup.

Beautiful flying! Hard to believe that not far away, on those superb slopes, was the terrible Kakoda Trail.

Then there was what we came to call Bomber Day. On a hillside near our strip at Moresby, the famous old 19th Bomb Group, whose B-17s had escaped from the Philippines and done yeoman service out of northern Australia and Moresby, built an officers' club.

The Fifth Air Force had few of these in New Guinea, and the bomber boys designed this one with great enthusiasm—a shack, low and unobtrusive, yet big enough for 40 men to get noisily drunk in comfort. It had a galvanized steel roof.

Steve knew one of the "truck drivers" from his university, so he was invited to take a look before the place opened. He brought Ben and me. I remember a mural behind the bar, depicting, cartoon-style, a view of New Guinea as seen from the altitude that a bomber pilot considered safe. That meant being high enough to see San Francisco's Golden Gate Bridge. It was a funny mural and as soon as its paint dried, the club was due to open.

On the morning of opening day, I was off-duty, trying to sleep late, but drowsily aware of a recurring aircraft noise, the rumble of a multiengine plane flying over our area at regular intervals. I was attuned to the sound of early missions taking off, and slept right through them, but this was annoying—too late for a mission to be leaving, too early for its return.

Then Ben stuck his head into the tent. "Come on out and look," he said. "We got a B-17 in trouble."

I was banging my boots and shaking out my shorts in a flash, and was outside in under 10 seconds. Here came the Fortress in a wide orbit at 2000 feet that took it right over us. One wheel down. Clearly, the gear had failed at takeoff, and the crew could neither retract that wheel nor lower the other.

"I guess they're burning up fuel," Ben said. "Then they'll bring it in."

"I hope they got rid of the bomb load," I said.

"Probably out at sea," said Ben. "Be a lot of dead fish out there."

We walked down to the Farmhouse and I cadged a cup of coffee. Canuck had been fooling with the dial of our battery-run radio, and had tuned in the bomber's frequency. It was a 19th Bomb Group plane.

Suddenly Canuck called out, "They're going to set the controls and jump!" He dashed outside. A bunch of us piled into a jeep and drove to the hillside overlooking our strip. Here we had a fine view of the big plane with its dangling wheel, lumbering overhead.

A tiny dark blob appeared beside it, falling away from it—a little scratch in the canvas of the sky. It tumbled down until a white circle abruptly bloomed above it. The first parachute. Others followed, and we counted them carefully:…eight… nine…ten. That left only one, the first pilot. He swung the plane onto a straight course, north, toward the mountains. We watched as he turned again, heading back toward us, and the sea beyond us, straight and level. "This'll be it," someone said. "He'll jump right here."

He did. His miniature figure flung itself out of the nose section, legs spread as it fell clear. The 'chute popped and he swung in his straps over our heads.

Then the pilotless plane began to turn!

"My God," said Canuck. "An engine's gone dry."

We could see one propeller windmilling uselessly. With two engines on the left and one on the right, the Fortress swung into a wide spiral—right over an area that held a dozen camps, including ours and the 19th Bomb Group's. It was as though the bomber had chosen to die at home.

No one could do a thing except watch. The plane now steadily lost altitude as it circled. Twice it came dangerously close to its own pilot as he yanked at his shrouds to change the direction of his painfully slow descent. At last we saw him land safely, not far away, and scramble to his feet to watch the bomber.

It was now too low to finish its last orbit. It would hit the next ridge. And we all realized that on the crest of that next ridge was the 19th Bomb Group's new officer's club, ready to open that night.

Inexorably, the huge plane thundered low over our heads and bore down on the shiny new corrugated roof of that beautiful club. It aimed at it as though someone was still at the controls. It was there! NOW!...But somehow it got past. It vanished beyond the ridge and then a swirling cloud of black smoke puffed into the sky, followed by a faint, metallic crunch. There wasn't enough fuel to produce a decent explosion. With uncanny precision, the huge Fortress crashed in the only couple of acres for miles that had no tents, no people, no supply dump, nothing.

The 19th had their opening that night. People who went said the club was fine—except for a long dent in the roof where the drooping wheel of the doomed bomber had *brushed* it that morning.

There was Lombardi. Tall for a fighter pilot, dark-haired, brown-skinned, with a quick flash of white teeth when he smiled, this guy had stepped right out of a recruiting poster. He was also bright, funny, kind, and modest. He'd graduated from Cornell, talked articulately, read books, and played talented baseball when we braved the heat to get up a five-inning game. When something got broken, like the belly-tank shower at the flight line, Lombardi would quietly fix it before anyone had a chance to yell for an aviation mechanic to come and mess with it.

Understandably, Lombardi was considered a great addition at the evening meal when the officers joked and argued with noisy amiability at their own long table, and around the poker table, afterward. At our daily task, he was competent, except for one thing which he couldn't help: He was dogged by bad luck.

One afternoon as he was slow-timing a plane, Lombardi's engine quit. He'd been flying west from Moresby along the coast, exploring an area we barely knew because we never needed to fly over it. When his prop stopped he had about 7000 feet between him and the shoreline. He glided down, over the long, wet mudflats reaching out into the Arafura Sea, found one spot that looked more solid, and bailed out over it.

Once he was out of the airplane, Lombardi's luck returned. He landed on a small coastal clearing—you couldn't really call it a beach—that indeed was solid and even had a track leading away from it, inland. So he rolled up his parachute as best he could, gathered his gear, and set out along this little path. In five minutes he reached a clearing with a house and some shacks around it, and even a flagpole with the Australian flag flying. It was a small mission station, and when he knocked on the front door, an astonished white man appeared, and offered him a cup of tea. He politely accepted and ended up staying a couple of weeks.

Lombardi, naturally, made friends with everyone, fixed a faulty generator, outlined the world situation neatly to the missionary and his wife, and helped teach the Papuan kids. He became the most popular person at the mission, and it was only reluctantly that the missionary used his Lombardi-fixed radio to ask for someone to come and take this magnificent stranger away.

A rescue boat showed up a few days later, anchored offshore, and sent in a rubber dinghy. Lombardi stepped aboard it. The entire mission stood on the shore to wave to him. And all the kids sang "Far Above Cayuga's Waters," which is Cornell's beautiful old song. Lombardi had taught it to them.

Some weeks later, while returning from a Wau milk run which I wasn't on, Lombardi called in his leader to say his coolant temperature was in the red and climbing, and he was getting smoke in the cockpit. The Beavers were over one of those deep, mysterious valleys, mist-shrouded in the mornings, then lusciously green to look down upon. It was there that Lombardi bailed out, his flight circling him as he went down. They said he waved from the parachute, and they kept with him until he landed. He seemed to be fine, standing tall and waving that he was OK.

Everyone knew the map coordinates and Beaver Leader, whoever it was that day, called them in to Maple, the Moresby sector. They sent a Cub next morning, which managed to land in the valley. The pilot hunted everywhere and could find no sign of life. Two more Cubs went in the next day and the pilots searched. Nothing.

We conjectured that Lombardi might have set up a little empire in that fertile valley. Perhaps he did. We never saw him again.

When we called Maple on our radios, we were usually answered by an Australian voice that grew familiar to us. But sometimes, as in a scramble, we got an American voice. Flyers—both American and Australian—did duty at "sector" as liaison officers. When my turn came, I found it a two-week cram course in radar and communications, even in making command decisions.

Here was a different world from the flight line and the Farmhouse. I was stationed in a Queensland-style house, closed and darkened inside, quiet except for the whir of fans. My desk overlooked a rudimentary "command room," with an outline map on a display board where airmen diagrammed flights of planes and radar blips. This was a small version of the room in London that Churchill visited during the Battle of Britain.

Churchill wouldn't have wasted much time here during my two weeks as sector officer. Not enough happened. But I learned the importance of following sector's orders, of not clogging the airwaves with chatter, of making the necessary calls clearly and calmly.

One stormy afternoon, toward the end of my shift, a call came from a P-38 flight, late in returning from a patrol. The weather was gloomy and miserable, showers blotting out the steep hillsides around the Moresby strips. The flight leader checked in with us and said the visibility was lousy but that they should make it into 14-Mile Strip without too much sweat.

Two of them did—the first element. Then a gust of rain swept over, the ceiling lowered, and the second element pulled up and went into a broad orbit to try again. The rain thundered down on our roof; the darkness increased.

The element leader called. They were still orbiting, just above the clouds. but they wanted a radio fix so they could tell where they were. I got on the radio to him and told him to fly straight and count to 20. He did it, calmy, slowly, and we got a triangulation on the voice and I gave him a course to fly and a safe altitude. He obeyed perfectly.

There was silence for a moment, then his voice: "Maple, from Outcast Blue Three: I've got a hole and I'm going down."

I acknowledged, and called the control tower at his strip to tell them. They said they could hear him, close overhead, then they could see his lights, and they lit the strip.

"Thank you, Maple," they said. "He's down safely."

"What about his wingman?" I asked.

"Not down yet," they said.

"Outcast Blue Four, this is Maple," I said into the mike. "Give us a call, please. Over."

No answer. The element leader's voice came in: "Maple, this is Outcast Blue Three, on the ground. Blue Four was with me as we started down. Over."

"Roger, Blue Three. Outcast Blue Four, this is Maple. Do you read me? Over."

No answer.

It was a scene right out of those good old flying movies like *Ceiling Zero*. But this was no movie. It was monotonous and awful and endless. And it had no happy ending. Outcast Blue's Number Four man—tail-ass Charlie—vanished in the night. Radar couldn't pick him up. He was too low.

A phone call came in from distant 17-Mile Strip. They'd heard a plane fly over in the rain and dark. It seemed to be heading for the mountains.

Not a sign of it was found. I suppose it may be one of those strange, forgotten wrecks that are still spotted from the air in that impossible country. Maybe, sometime in the past few decades, it was reported. Maybe aviation archeologists will come down on it with a helicopter and haul away bits for a museum.

Fine. But a bit too late for Outcast Blue Four.

Finally, there's the story of our last Moresby scramble. The day's work had ended, and Kelvin was already standing naked under our belly-tank shower, with sun-warm water rinsing off the laundry soap. I was standing by to take my turn. I'd piled my gear on a cot inside the shack.

Thank God I still had my boots on. For suddenly the operations clerk shouted, "Scramble! All planes! Angels Twenty! Over the area!"

We were really caught short this time, dashing for our holsters and flying suits, bumping into one another, cursing, stumbling on the cots. I got aboard a jeep with one leg still outside my flying suit. Kelvin simply wrapped a towel around his waist and hopped on.

Despite the surprise, we got off the ground pretty fast and started climbing as steeply as the little beasts would go. Maple seemed excited. They were seeing firm, hard blips, surely aircraft this time. We followed their directions carefully, staggering up to 20,000 feet and mushing around on the vectors they gave us. But we saw nothing.

It was beautiful up there, the sun low, but still bright, washing our planes with golden light. But at 20,000 feet it's not very warm. We all worried about Kelvin. "How're you doing, Otto?" someone said.

"They're about to freeze off," he answered.

We stooged around for a few minutes, then the sector called. "Beaver, from Maple, target is heading back north. Come on home."

So it *had* been something, after all. Perhaps a Dinah, perhaps a bomber hoping to catch us with an evening raid. Perhaps they'd spotted us clawing up toward them in the sunset, and had peeled away. Perhaps we'd earned our pay that day.

Down we came. The ground below was very dark, for down there the sun had set and the tropical night had started. To use what light remained, we spiraled steeply, losing altitude as quickly as we could. And as our planes, chilled by the cold of 20,000 feet, met the still-warm air of 5000 feet, we fogged up.

Inside the windscreen of the P-39 was a slab of armor glass, beautifully machined, maybe a couple of inches thick, and perfectly flat, so there was a gap between it and the curved windscreen. And there was no way to get your hand into that gap.

When the armor glass fogged, we all quickly wiped the inside surface clear. But we couldn't get at the other surface, and we couldn't see. Flying by looking out the side windows, we kept sinking into the gloom, and very soon we were not only fogged up, but in the dark as well.

To our credit, we didn't start panicking on the radio, though I think everyone was as scared as I was. Formation was forgotten, but we all clung together in a folorn hope that someone could see what he was doing. Someone said, "Get the lights on," and I realized I hadn't a clue where the light switches were. I'd never used them. Watching the plane to my left out of my window. I groped for a switch I could see in memory. I snapped it, wondering what the hell it might do.

On came a bright light in the cockpit, that dazzled me. Quickly I spotted the running lights switch and snapped them on and the cockpit light off. But of course all I could see for a few moments was a brilliant blue blob on my retina.

In strange, terrified silence, we descended into the dark, groping between the hills that we knew were there. Blind, helpless, I, for one, expected at any moment to smash into a hillside and explode. I was never so sure of approaching death, and I hate to say it, but instead of my life flashing through my head, instead of thoughts of the hereafter, I just felt angry and stupid and frustrated that my hard-gained competence was of no use in this situation.

I didn't have the gall to pray to an overworked God. After all, God's own physical laws make fog inevitable when warm air suddenly meets cold glass. How could God reverse this carefully designed procedure? Instead of praying, I swore like any good air force pilot: "Damn, Damn, Damn," again and again. Probably what the Light Brigade muttered, riding for the Russian guns, and what Custer said when the Sioux came down upon him at the Little Big Horn.

With incredible luck, and perhaps a little more skill than any of us realized we had—and maybe a nod from God—every one of us landed safely and smoothly. We met in the alert shack, lit by some candles and the ops clerk's flashlight. We were all there, Kelvin shivering in his towel. We didn't say anything. We just looked at one another in some wonder, and with a certain fondness. Then we all left for the Farmhouse, all piling into two jeeps, all keeping close together.

CHAPTER
EIGHT

A HERO IN SYDNEY

A lot of strange things happened to me in June 1943, and all came as a surprise. On a breathlessly humid late afternoon, just as we were relaxing in the alert shack, finished with our missions and beginning to gather up the cards and paperback novels, Jeff appeared and read off a few names, including mine. We looked up a little anxiously. "You men get to your tents right now and get into uniform," said Jeff. "Then report back here on the double. General Wurtsmith's here, and he wants to decorate you."

He left us gaping. Decorate? I figured it must be squadron slang for something, a stern berating, perhaps, for our utter uselessness, or maybe for specific sins—in my case, getting a United States aircraft shot to ribbons.

Ben, who was on duty with me that day, was just as puzzled. "I don't know what it's all about," he said as we hitched a jeep ride to our tent. "I just thought it meant getting a medal."

Steve was in the tent, already wearing a mildewed, but clean khaki shirt, and was rubbing green mold off his creased khaki pants—unworn for three months. "It is a medal," he said. "Air medals. Ordinarily they just go on your record, but Wurtsmith happened to be here."

"What the hell are we getting air medals for?" I asked, rummaging in my footlocker.

"Eating crap instead of food," suggested Ben.

He was about right. The citation, when it was added to our orders, read "for operational flight missions from March 10 to May 7, 1943." During that period, it turned out, I had flown 25 "combat missions." That designation was pretty arbitrary, but in essence a combat mission was one in which "hostile contact was probable and expected." We were being repaid, sort of, for all the adrenalin we had pumped during those endless, tedious, frustrating, flights over Wau.

We got dressed and returned to the flight line where Wurtsmith, C.O. of Fifth Fighter Command, was kidding around with Jeff and Guthrie and Heming. He was just one of them, a young fellow with a little mustache, with command pilot wings on his chest and a star on his shoulders. Jeff broke away and came over. "You guys look pretty sharp," he said. "Line up here, why don't you, facing out at the strip. And no laughing. This is serious business."

The general approached, and we popped to attention. He smiled at us affably, read us the citation, and called out names. "Good to have you with us," he said as he pinned my little blue-and-gold ribbon on my shirt. "Keep up the good work."

Then we were dismissed, and went up to the Farmhouse for a drink. "Got your Junior Birdman's Badge, I see," said John G., making room at the bar. The phrase brought back memories of various adventure series I'd followed on late-afternoon radio when I was 12 or so. "Send in ten boxtops of Whiz-Bang cereal," the announcer would enthuse, "and you'll get a Junior Birdman's Badge!" And with a modest glimmer of enlightenment, I understood why I'd heard old pilots speak of missions as "boxtops."

"How many of these medals have you got?" I asked John G.

He shrugged. "God knows. Three or four I guess. I think they stop keeping count when you've got more than a hundred missions."

"Why do they do this? Aren't medals supposed to mean something?"

"Some of them do. And remember that twenty-five missions means a hell of a lot when you're flying over Europe. Used to be that way here too. Maybe, someday, it'll be that way again. But for now, just figure your ribbon might make your Mom feel better, back home. And for God's sake don't wear it when you go on leave. Medals really mean something in Australia."

It was more and more evident that we were caught in a strange, still backwater of war. "I think the Nips kissed off Moresby with your raid," Steve said one evening. He always called it my raid. "They're not going to mess with this place any more. I think that as long as we stay here life will be pretty dull."

As usual, Steve was right. But at least we got a break from the boredom. Leave policy for pilots was ten days off for every three months of duty, and our batch of replacements all became eligible at once. Doug Horachov and I were ordered to Sydney. Steve and Ben would follow after we got back. Then Shriver would go with an old pilot.

Looking back, I don't think I deserved that first leave. I needed more learning time, more combat, more hours in the air. Doug said he felt the same way. But of course, when the orders came we went happily south, and the impact of Sydney was so strange that I guess we needed it after all.

It took forever to get there. The C-47 trudged southward above the tropical clouds and then at last above a red, brown, green, yellow landscape, nearly empty of any notable feature or sign of life. We read, and dozed, and stared out the windows. And after hours of this we felt pressure increase on our eardrums, and realized that the plane was letting down.

Below were buildings and roads. Then a huge, sprawling harbor in the midst of red roofs, green parklands marked by long, straight patches in the grass. Cricket pitches. We remembered them from Queensland. Then we were on final, wheels down, flaps down, nose up, squish, rumble. So this is Sydney.

We'd no sooner cut off the engines than the door opened and a girl stuck her head in. "Welcome to Sydney," she said. "Go straight through to a big room...." Hell, I can't remember what she said. All I remember was that she was a real girl. She looked like a girl, and talked like one, and she was perfectly beautiful, and I loved her. Doug said he did too.

Clutching our bags, we trooped off the plane and into a huge, confusing room. Seated at a desk, another girl, just as wonderful as the first, gave us chits with which to buy cigarettes and booze at a special price, and asked us where we wanted to go. I told her the squadron flat was Onslow Gardens.

"Not far from the Cross," said the girl. "You can share a taxi with these men"—she indicated three other pilots looking bewildered—"and don't let the driver charge you more than..." whatever it was. I decided that I loved her. Doug said he saw her first.

We were about to leave when she handed each of us a small packet. "You might possibly need these," she said. We thanked her and left. We glanced into the packages. Condoms. Wow!

We'd been well briefed about Sydney by the old pilots, and had promised not to disgrace the squadron by having noisy orgies in the flat and throwing up in the beds, or by being rude to the landlady who had mothered the whole gang back in the Bankstown days. We knew we mustn't talk about how great we were and what a lot of heavy action we'd been through, because the Australians had been through five times as much and knew "great" when they saw it. We'd also been told that with a little know-how and a lot of luck, we each ought to find a ravishing Australian girl to sleep with.

Well, Doug and I soon discovered that the glorious days when Yanks were sexually assaulted by Sydney girls were over. By June 1943, Americans were everywhere. Generals and "chicken colonels," all spiffed up in creased pants and beribboned tunics, seemed to step out of every taxi with ravishing Australian girls on their arms. We met one of these couples just as we reached our flat, that first day, still shivering in the unaccustomed cold of the south. We stared at them, and they stared back, coldly, the colonel waiting for a salute, the ravishing Australian girl wrinkling her nose at two scrawny, rumpled second lieutenants in mildewed khakis, and crinkled leather flight jackets.

We had hoped that our New Guinea clothes would exude an aura of glamour. But when we went inside and introduced ourselves to Mrs. Thomas, the landlady, she made it clear that the only thing they exuded was the aroma of mold. She made us take off our khakis immediately so she could put them in the wash. We broke out our "pinks and greens," the dove-gray whipcord pants, called "pinks," that U.S. Army officers wore back then, and the dark-green "blouse," with brass buttons. They were badly creased for having been stored so long in our footlockers, and Mrs. Thomas, seeing us come downstairs in them, took us into her flat and made us wait, hopping around pantless in front of her electric radiator, while she ironed them. Doug and I agreed that she was our Number One ravishing Australian girl.

We were at the right age—and certainly in the right job—to adapt quickly to swiftly changing environments. But the change from heavy heat to Sydney's rather mild winter temperature left us shivering with ague. And the feel of clean sheets instead of sweat-stiffened blankets, the taste of steak instead of "boeuf de boullie," the sound of busy streets instead of snarling skies, the sights and scents of real people, including women, instead of the same, endlessly worried young men, dressed in tropical tatters, waiting day after day for an olive-drab phone to ring so that they could risk their necks—all of that, all at once, rocked us back on our feet. It was as though we'd been struck by a tornado of civilization.

It took a day to adapt. Then that first leave became joyous. I've never been a huge toper, but I gave it a good shot, back then—enough to throw today's memories mercifully out of focus. I only vaguely remember the misadventures of two well-brought-up middle-class American boys trying to pick up snazzy blondes who looked cheap enough to say yes. I remember more clearly forming some solid friendships, eating wonderful food—but not very much of it, because our stomachs had shrunk—learning the way from Kings Cross to Pitt Street, going to great movies in palatial theaters and feeling the tension gradually leave, like heat ticking away from a turned-off stove.

I remember music on the radio, Cooper's beer, the terrible pale yellow eggnog with a Dutch name—Avocaat, I think—that the people at the special liquor mart always made us buy because it was the only booze they had plenty of. It was pretty sick-making, but we thinned it out with gin and choked it down. I remember uniforms everywhere—British and Dutch as well as Australian—and so damn many Americans that they were all trying to figure out ways of getting away from one another. We went to the theater, for example, because we thought most Americans wouldn't bother to. And it was jammed with Americans who thought the same thing.

The ten days went very quickly. Then we opened the big parachute bags we'd folded inside our luggage and crammed them with bottles of beer, salamis, cheese, crackers, fruit, anything we could get our hands on, to pass around the squadron. My most valuable present was a bottle of Scotch that I wangled from a bartender at enormous cost. It was for my crew chief, and I was following an old Air Corps tradition of a pilot expressing thanks to the person who held his life in his hands.

Then it was time to go "home." The word came to us naturally as we said good-by to Mrs. Thomas, and she smiled at it, and kissed us both.

TOKYO ROSE WAS RIGHT

At work again, we were conscious of heightening excitement. In great secrecy it was whispered that we were going to move. Many of our missions were now west of Wau and a little longer, over unknown hills that sometimes weren't mapped properly. We escorted transports to a distant valley where, apparently, engineers and light earth-moving equipment were being dropped by parachute. I can't vouch for that, because I never saw it through the intervening clouds. Anyway, our task was to search the air, not the ground. We knew that in this area the chance of interception was indeed "probable and expected," just as the Junior Birdman's citation read, and the more readily affrighted of us scanned the sky endlessly for the blazing attack that seemed sure to come.

The place we were flying over, where the airborne engineers were scraping away the kunai and shaping two dirt airstrips, was called Marilinan on our maps. It was in the Lower Watut Valley, well up in what we flyers considered "Nip country," and what the Australian infantry thought of as a pretty good spot for a rest camp. We maintained secrecy rigorously, quite proud of ourselves for being so careful, and then Tokyo Rose blew the whistle on us.

We used to listen to her often in the Farmhouse, because she had the latest records—Benny Goodman, Tommy Dorsey, Glenn Miller, Artie Shaw—and played them for 20 minutes at a time before giving us a little talk about how the wives and sweethearts of us "nice American boys" were all sleeping with draft dodgers and "Four Effers" (guys who were classified

4-F—unacceptable—by the draft board). Then she'd say the same thing to the Australians, only it was the Americans who were sleeping with their wives and sweethearts. "And greetings to you brave Diggers of the AIF. I'm sorry about all that malaria in the New Guinea jungles. You really should keep out of there and get back to your Sheilas before the Yanks get them all pregnant. Wouldn't it be good to be on the road to Gundegai again? Or lying on the beach at Bondi?"

This time she gave us a terrific Glenn Miller concert, good enough so we stopped chattering, and when she began her spiel we were all listening. "Greetings to the veteran pilots of the Thirty-fifth Fighter Group," she said, "who are getting ready to move to Marilinan. We have a fine reception waiting for you."

So thanks to Tokyo Rose we now knew for sure that our squadron and the 40th were going to move. We knew the 39th would stay because the strips being built in the kunai weren't long enough to take P-38s. We all looked at one another, then giggled helplessly and poured another drink.

The reception started soon after. It was another standard mission, escorting C-47s on a supply drop at Marilinan, only now we officially called the place Tsili-Tsili. That was apparently an alternate name—most places in New Guinea seemed to have them—or it might have been the exact spot where the strips were being built. Anyway, it was comforting to know that Tokyo Rose had said we were going to Marilinan, and actually we were going to Tsili-Tsili.

We were all flying two missions a day, because we needed that new base, and so far the weather was good. I was on the early mission one bright morning, two flights humming serenely around the target area, nothing in the bright sky but us. Our ground-hugging transports dropped their cargoes of food and equipment and then headed for the barn, and we were well above them, weaving to stay with them on the return. We soon passed the next mission, Beaver's other two flights essing above their pod of loaded biscuit bombers, preparing for their drop.

A few words broke radio silence: "Beaver White from Red, got you."

"Got you too, Red."

We continued homeward, lulled by the wavering hiss in our earphones, as familiar as the gentle break of ripples on a stony beach.

Then, shockingly, our radios erupted.

"Drop your tanks, Beaver!"

Then a disjointed gabble of voices and long periods of silence:

"Behind you, Jamie!"

....

"Left! Left!"..."I'm on him!"..."Damn!"

....

"Get that bastard!"

....

And, chillingly, "You OK, Willie...? Willie...? *Get out of it, Willie!*"

....

But Willie Vosburgh didn't get out of it. We eight pilots in Red and Yellow flights landed at Moresby, had smoko, rested, and were out beside the strip when White and Blue swept over the strip with that whistling sound that came from the tape being blown off their gun muzzles. The Airacobras looked lean and pretty without their belly tanks. But there were only six of them.

They landed and taxied back, and one suddenly halted, right on the strip, its engine dead, its prop wheeling to a stop.

A truck went out to it, and an ambulance, but the pilot was OK. Mendoza. A new guy. He'd taken some shots in his engine. A bullet had cut an oil line, and the Allison finally froze up after getting him home.

Willie Vosburgh had bought it, they told us. He was an older pilot, thin and tired and quiet. And when he slid away from the others and they called him, he never answered, never said anything, just sank quietly, wearily into the hills and exploded.

Burnham was the other missing man. He was a new guy, a North Carolinian, big for a fighter pilot, and friendly and likable. They'd seen him bail out and thought he'd reached a hilltop safely. But no one was sure. They'd all been pretty busy.

A formation of Sallys, Japanese light bombers, had arrived at Tsili-Tsili at the same time as our transports, and Red and Yellow flights bounced them. Then the enemy fighters—Oscars—bounced our guys and bore down on our transports. So there was a big soiree up there in the wild hills.

We'd shot down three of theirs—two Sallys and one Oscar. One of our pilots, a replacement named Cahill, but always called Dink because he was so little, had clobbered the fighter and one of the bombers. Everyone had scored on the other Sally, but credit went to Canuck, who'd finished it off. For once we'd done better than the enemy. We'd killed about seven of them for only one of us. Possibly two. How Burnham was going to get off that hill was anyone's guess.

That was the way we scored it that evening, jabbering away over our whiskey. But we pretty quickly talked about other things, things in the future. No one wanted to dwell on Vosburgh, on the sudden ending of a decent, competent, private life.

I hit the sack that night with a troubled mind. I'd escaped another testing that day, thanks to being on the first mission—low on fuel—instead of the second. I was glad, sort of, but also frustrated. The chance had almost come to get into it again. How, I wondered, would I have made out this time?

Would I have taken a burst like Willie? I couldn't stop myself from picturing a load of Japanese metal crashing into me, cutting me almost in two as the light faded before my eyes. Was that how it would feel to enter infinity?

Sweat prickled on my body, and quickly I changed course, contemplating what I might have done to the enemy. Maybe I would have come through like Dink. Probably not, but still....Lying on my cot, I could feel myself rolling three-quarters over to wrench the nose of my plane down at a streaking Sally. I could see the enemy, dark green with outlined "meatballs." I could see the plexiglass canopy where the tail gunner was swinging on me....

I must shoot before his twin guns ripple with fire and he nails me like that guy in the Moresby raid. Get the sight ahead of him for deflection...more...a little more...NOW!

My body twisted and hunched as the hammer of guns echoed inside my head. I imagined flashes along the Sally's fuselage...a burst of smoke from an engine nacelle. And as the bomber slides toward the ground I glimpse a dainty, mottled Oscar flashing past, and with an easy swing I find the exact deflection and my beautifully aimed cannon shells blow him to smithereens. Another Oscar scuttles for a cloud to hide in, but I rip him with a short burst before dropping on yet another fleeing Sally....

Killer Park, the awed squadron calls me. "Ace in the Making" reads the headline in a *Life* magazine profile of me....

Pretty dumb. But better than thinking about Vosburgh. I fell asleep, guns ablaze, in the middle of a split-S.

We moved to Tsili-Tsili around the first of September 1943. I don't remember exactly, and I don't have it logged because I wasn't there. To facilitate the move, about eight of the pilots who were due for leave at roughly that time were sent south. Steve, Ben, and I were among them.

Sydney was more crowded than ever, more frantic. We ran into Guppy, whom we hadn't seen much of, and he was wonderfully entertaining and socially resourceful. His squadron flat wasn't far from ours, and sometimes, for a few minutes within the frantic days, the old trio, Guppy, Steve, and I, were alone together, talking.

Much to his own astonishment, Guppy had turned out to be a very good pilot, and his plane, the P-38 Lightning, was proving itself the perfect weapon with which to battle the Zero. "The secret is the climb," he told us. "A 'Thirty-eight can indicate three hundred in a shallow climb, and none of their fighters can do that. They can go fast, all right, when they're straight and level or in a dive, and they can climb straight up. They can hang on their props, for crying out loud. But they can't stay with us when we climb away. So while they spin around in circles and loops, trying to get us into a dogfight, we just go straight through and then climb away. Hold three hundred on the clock and shoot every time you see a meatball— that's how to fight a Zero."

"You can't do that on a P-39," Steve said.

"That's why I'm surprised you guys are still alive."

Guppy had already shot down a plane, and seemed sure to tangle with more, since his missions were far longer than ours. He loved the P-38—"It turns like a truck," he admitted, "but it's fast, and you don't fight torque in it, and it's a nice feeling to hide between those two big engines when the bullets are flying."

And then Guppy was gone from us, holding to his own frenetic pace from bar to bed and back.

We went "home" again, with a kiss from Mrs. Thomas and parachute bags crammed for our "family." And this time we landed at Moresby, then hopped another transport up to Tsili-Tsili. The squadron was barely there, but the move was typical air force—quick, efficient, complete. Our tent at Moresby had been struck, all our gear packed (mostly by ourselves), and the whole shebang set up again at Tsili, tent raised, cots in place with blankets and air mattresses, footlockers and barracks bags all there, not one item missing.

But how strange to find our trappings in a gloomy, damp world far beneath a canopy of giant trees, among twisting vines and marshy gullies. The dark-green tents rose as randomly as mushrooms on the black forest duff. Paths wound past the great root-buttressed trunks, linking our canvas dwellings and leading to a big mess tent with long deal tables and benches for everyone. Its garish lightbulbs blazed and faded with the uncertain health and nourishment of the gasoline generator puttering incessantly, outside.

We opened our parachute bags for the delectation of our friends, and they munched and guzzled happily, and told us we should have been here when it was rough. That was a ritual saying, back then, along with "Didja get any?" when a man landed from a soiree or returned from leave.

We caught up on the news. Jeff, our old C.O., had been sent to Group Headquarters, leaving the squadron to Guthrie, who had been operations officer. Guthrie had supervised our move, but it was up to Steve, Ben, and me to make something of our tent. Ideally, that meant building a floor. With all that rain forest we had wood enough, but no tools to get at it. And the breathless air and drenching humidity made physical endeavor unattractive. We made do with a tarpaulin spread on the forest floor.

All sorts of small bugs still found their way into the tents. One in particular showed up everywhere—small, black, and furry. When it crawled on your skin it left a slight rash that itched. And if you smacked the thing and crushed it, it got back at you with a powerful and distinctive odor—pure American skunk.

The smell of these ubiquitous little bugs—"skunk bugs," we quickly called them—held a strange nostalgia for us. I used to wake up sometimes in the night, sure that I was back in New Hampshire because I'd rolled on a skunk bug. Others had vivid dreams of home when that happened. Some crushed the little things deliberately for sentimental reasons.

Skunk bugs weren't all. One night, inspecting my sleeping bag routinely with my flashlight before climbing in, I found a very small snake, perhaps a foot long. Harmless? Who knows? Ben barely escaped getting drilled by a scorpion on his shirt collar. We all were dank and filthy much of the time, and our clothes rotted, the leather turning green, the cloth giving way if you poked a finger at it. Our skin rotted, too, especially under arms and between legs where rashes always eventually won their endless battles with Doctor Mac's ointments. He'd put us on atabrine instead of quinine, now, and watched us carefully as we turned yellow. But the stuff kept malaria at a minimum.

"Doc," Steve asked him one day, "will atabrine make us sterile?"

"We'll see," he said.

Naturally, we moaned about our hardships. But down deep we liked the glamour of a forward air base, and quickly understood the reason for our being here. No sooner had we moved than MacArthur pulled off his paratroop drop on Nadzab. Our planes stooged around with all the other Fifth Air Force fighters, safeguarding the great man while he flew over the operation at a marvelous height. Masses of C-47s dumped enough paratroopers to capture New York City. They didn't have much trouble taking over this part of the Markham Valley, which, it turned out, was defended by three or four Japanese soldiers. But MacArthur, looking down from on high was, according to General Kenney, "jumping up and down like a kid" at the grandeur of his triumph.

The Markham Valley drop was a beginning of the long-awaited tide turning in the Pacific. For MacArthur to make his much-advertised "Return," the troops in New Guinea had to recapture places where the Japanese were firmly entrenched. Lae came first. We would support the Diggers as they drove on it and on Salamaua. Then would come Rabaul. This big enemy base on New Britain, carved out of volcanic heights, would require heavy bombing, and the bombers would need long-range escorts—P-38s. On their way home, the Lightnings would refuel at our base while we patrolled overhead to keep the Japanese from taking advantage of a beautiful target opportunity.

The list of places to be recaptured went on and on: Finschafen, Madang, Alexishafen, Uligan Harbour, Bogia, Hansa Bay, then the terrible Sepik River country that led to mighty Wewak with its fleets of bombers and swarms of Oscars and now Tonys, the new Japanese fighters designed like the German Me-109. And beyond Wewak lay Hollandia, another Rabaul. Hell, the war was just *beginning*. "Golden Gate in 'forty-eight" was the most optimistic of our forecasts. It was a lot better than "Home alive in 'fifty-five."

Soon after we settled in at Tsili-Tsili, Burnham, who had bailed out during the great soiree, showed up. In the fight, an Oscar had clobbered him from behind, and the P-39's rear-mounted engine had taken all the metal. The Allison saved Burnham's life, but quit in the process. Unhurt, he shucked the door, rolled out, pulled the D-ring, and two seconds after the 'chute popped, he landed in the short highland grass.

He bundled up all that silk and sat down on it to have a cigarette and think things over. He said it was very hot and still and peaceful. No sound except the distant snarl of aircraft. It was *too* still; He was sure someone was watching him. He finished his cigarette, snubbed it out, rose and detached his escape kit, moving slowly and deliberately. He also unsnapped the strap that held his Colt in the shoulder holster. There was so little wind that the pale-blue cloud of tobacco smoke still hung over him.

And abruptly, he found himself staring at about a dozen very small brown people, wearing hardly anything. They simply appeared at the edge of his clearing and came carefully toward him carrying long spears. But he saw that they were looking more at the tobacco smoke than at him. So he sat back down and lit another cigarette, and they stopped and stared. And he grinned at them between puffs, and they grinned back....

Well, the upshot was that he gave the pygmies all his cigarettes and showed them how to light up, thus corrupting them for good. And when he made it clear, by gestures (Pidgin didn't work), that he wanted to get off the hilltop, they showed him a trail, affably enough. He packed his gear and started down, turning back once to wave good-by. "I think they raised their hands back at me," he said, "but there was so much cigarette smoke by then that they were kind of fogged out."

So Burnham got back, thanks to an Australian patrol down in the valley. The Aussies flew him to Moresby, where he was checked over. Nothing wrong, except a cigarette cough, so here he was back home. Burnham was later consulted by a Sydney anthropologist who had been shown the intelligence report of his experience and managed to talk his way up to New Guinea and wangle a flight to our squadron. He asked Burnham a lot of questions about the pygmies. Burnham was very pleased to have done something really useful.

We hadn't given a thought to the natives around Tsili. We knew that our laundryman, Jerry, was very far away from his friends at Moresby, and knew no one here except Snowball, the laundry boy for the 40th Squadron. He'd ride over to the 40th on his bike—we'd flown it up from Moresby for him—squelching along the muddy tracks. Then the two would gossip and sing hymns in harmony and laugh together. I remember passing the two of them in a jeep one evening as we headed up to camp from the flight line, sweaty and grimy and tired. They stepped to the side of the track and both popped to attention and snapped a beautiful British Empire salute at us, hands flat and quivering, teeth gleaming in a broad grin as we cheered them.

And then some official from ANGAU caught up with them. They were too far from their territory. They'd have to return to Moresby. We'd always liked and admired the guys from ANGAU: big, husky Aussies who knew the jungle like a book and had given us tips on survival. But we didn't want to lose Jerry—he was part of our family—and we swore at the rules and damned the whole system. Guthrie argued with ANGAU, but as he explained to us, this was an Australian matter and we had no right to interfere with Australian affairs.

One day a whole community of natives traversed our camp, village leaders in front, warriors carrying spears and forming a guard for a strange-looking albino who must have been considered sacred. The women, loaded like mules with all the baggage of this village, took up the rear, with the children and a few dogs.

They walked right through us, along our paths, past our tents, silent and intent, until they were gone. We stared in astonishment, in some dismay at this blatant trespass. Then we realized that this spot we had settled and had come to think of as *ours* was really far more *theirs*.

We began adjusting to the jungle and even came to pride ourselves on learning something about it. Foxey Shriver, who'd studied botany at college, taught us how to identify breadfruit trees. We knew we could eat that rather tasteless fruit if we bailed out. We looked for birds that might be edible, and once I drew an army carbine from ordnance and joined a hunt for wild pigs.

We had no luck, but found the carbine delightfully light and accurate. The army thought it lacked wallop, but we considered making it part of our escape kit, for with it you could hit a bird without destroying the meat. Of course it was too big, but Ferguson, with a lot of help from an armorer, managed to cut one down and give it a clip-on stock so it would fit rather bulkily in his pack. I think some units adopted this idea later on. It always surprised and pleased us that so many of our hasty notions of making life a little more permanent were actually picked up and acted on by grave and dutiful military planners.

Hunting alternate foods became important because our rations were worse than ever, and sometimes failed to arrive at all. For ten days in a row, our valley was lost in either dense fog or endless heavy rain. No C-47 could see the strips for a landing, or even find the place for a drop, and we ate only hard tack—more and more weevily every day—and peanut butter. We had can after can of peanut butter because of a mistaken order some time before, and now it rescued us. I've liked the stuff ever since.

There was no flying during that time. We went down to the line faithfully every day and after staring at the weather, we'd simply read and talk and play baseball in the rain. We talked about our lives before the war, in college, or struggling to get along in miserable Depression jobs—or the even more miserable lack of them. Steve had been working in his father's real estate business. Briker had been trying to sell typewriters. Schriver had helped with his family ranch. Horachov and I had both started to teach school. Most of the old pilots cared for nothing beyond the field of flying. They had joined the old Air Corps for careers in it, and there they would stay.

We agreed with them that staying after the war ended might be the best choice for many of us. The Army Air Forces would at long last become the United States Air Force, a distinction that may seem trivial, but was important to all of us. We figured that this USAF ought to be able to put a man on the moon in 25 years—the late 1960s. We were convinced that our country would be a new empire, by then, powerful enough to run the world with justice and fairness and decency and all that other good stuff. It would be sort of a welfare state, we guessed, but with a good chance for our own private enterprises. The president would doubtless be a woman.

We dripped idealism with every word. But we also saw the need for force—particularly in the air. So staying in the new USAF made sense.

Our dreams hurried the pace of time, but didn't improve the weather. One 40th Squadron pilot, determined to get in the air during a short break in the clouds, started up his plane and eased forward toward the strip. Immediately, his nose wheel sank into mud, he swerved, and the propeller struck a small boundary light at the edge of the strip, lobbing it 100 feet into the air. Mired down, prop bent, the pilot shamefacedly waited for a tractor to tow him away. We Beavers, watching from our alert tent, were sorry when the diversion was over. We had to make do then with two dogs copulating in the renewed rain.

I noticed a thing I'd read about—that when life becomes very hard, people improve their treatment of one another. During those starving days, we all seemed to like one another more, to laugh with crazy enjoyment at silly jokes and sayings, to share a special warmth, a true affection.

CHAPTER
TEN

SKUNK BUGS OF
TSILI-TSILI

Our whiskey ration took it heavy during the starving time. Since we had no Farmhouse, no friendly pilots' bar, each four-man tent in the pilots' area was customarily issued one bottle of whiskey every ten days. That amounted to two ounces per day per pilot. Slim pickings, indeed, but fortunately many of the pilots were still only lads of 18 or 19, who had sworn on the family Bible, back in Iowa or Kansas, never to touch the stuff. Those of us who came from outside the Bible Belt and were free of any particular strictures were able to appeal to the clean livers and acquire their bottles. Thus we built up a small stock.

Pennsylvania rye whiskey, said the green label. When first in the squadron, I carefully avoided it the night before a mission. The world of Tsili-Tsili made me less careful. I just didn't give a damn if I flew with a hangover or not. A few deep breaths of oxygen worked wonders with last night's booze.

Many of the older pilots drank frequently. Heming had always downed enough to get quietly, privately smashed every night, yet flew with undiminished skill. Back at Moresby, where he had a tent with a raised floor, Heming used to wake in the wee hours, bladder bursting, roll to the left side of his cot, next to the edge of the floor, and pee out. One night he was sloshed enough to roll the wrong way. He filled one of his cherished Australian flying boots. It was a terrible mistake, rousing him to fury in the morning when he put it on. But later that same day I watched him fly inverted past our little

99

control tower so that John G. could film him on an 8-millimeter camera. John G. missed him the first time because he went by too fast. And when he told Heming on the radio, Heming rolled over again, upside-down, and came by the tower nose high, almost stalled out, and so low that John G. was looking down at him.

Heming had now been transferred to Red Flight, so I often flew with him. Before our weather turned sour, we flew close cover for the Diggers who made a landing at Finschafen, and I was Heming's element leader. We were there at dawn, flying over the swarm of landing craft that churned toward the beach. We were sure we'd see "bandits" on that early patrol, but it was the second patrol, not us, that hit them. No score, no losses.

Soon after, Heming led Red Flight on a routine patrol over the battle area. He was frustrated by missing a soiree during the landing, and not finding anyone to do battle with today, so suddenly he waggled his wings, the signal to close up on him.

We did. Then he gestured us into echelon. We all tacked onto his right. Down went his nose, and the four of us howled earthward toward a group of thatched huts a mile or so into the Japanese lines.

"Gunsights," said Heming tersely, and I realized he was going to strafe. It hadn't been ordered, but Heming was bored.

Whistling over the trees, we came on the houses. I lifted, then lowered the nose to get the sight on one, and realized anew that this was why the P-39 had been designed. Down here on the deck visibility was superb, control precise and instant. When I triggered it, the cannon thumped gloriously against my prostate. Timbers and roof flew; flames started. Heming hauled up and we followed him out of there, but Fisher, on my wing, started falling behind. "Beaver from Red Four," he called. "Wing trouble. Snafu."

"You OK?" I asked.

"Sure," he said, and peeled away for home. It turned out he had a coconut jammed in the leading edge of his right wing.

Satisfied with having vandalized some shacks that were probably empty, we clawed back to our patrol altitude. Then a call came from sector: "Bandits headed into coast at Angels

Twenty." The radar put them near us. Heming started a climb, and we two remaining acolytes followed suit, pouring on the coal to get all the way up there. I remember giving my gas gauge a critical look, and then in a burst of recklessness putting it out of mind.

Around went the altimeter needle: 10,000, 15, 17, then slowly to 18 and painfully toward 19. And, magically, a blob of planes appeared, still above us, moving inland over the coast, their course neatly closing with ours.

We saw six bombers in two vees, probably Lilys, judging from their size. Their undersides were off-white—hard to see against the sky, except for the brilliant red circles. Above them, maybe 1000 feet higher, the Zeroes swarmed, at least a dozen of them in pairs, weaving in a tangle of gleaming, dainty forms. The whole formation was moving very quickly above us, not quite in range, soon to be out of it completely as they bore toward the battle area.

We dropped our tanks, wrenched our lightened planes upward, and I guess we all took a shot together. I know I almost stood on my tail to get the whole mess of bombers entering my sight, then blasted away. Tracers looped up toward those pale, elusive shapes, but many of the arcing lines of machine gun fire fell short. Perhaps a few of our cannon shells reached among the enemy. For though we saw no hits, the six Lilys swung neatly around and headed away. We three miserable Airacobras had driven them off!

But...hold everything...here came the fighters!

We saw the glint of sunlight on them as they all rolled on their backs at once, up above the fleeing bombers. Then their noses swung down right at us, getting bigger fast as they dove. The outlines of all those slender wings suddenly rippled with flame. They had opened fire.

I think the three of us reacted the same way at the same time. I know that the sight of those attacking Zeroes was enough for me. I was almost stalled out anyway, probably about to spin, and I simply throttled back, ruddered the plane straight, popped the stick forward, and as she started a clean dive, crammed the throttle open as far as it would go.

Now the P-39 was doing the thing it did best of all—heading for the ground, fast. I looked around at the pursuit. The enemy planes were still coming, their guns still ablaze all along their wings. But they were falling back. A tracer or two flashed past me, but I knew I'd lost them.

My little plane was screaming toward the sea as if to find refuge in that cobalt-blue water. I eased off the power and pressed the stick back. The nose swung cleanly upward, and my cheeks sagged, my jaw fell open, and vision misted away in my bulging eyes. Clamping my stomach muscles and grunting, I got the blood back to my head and looked around.

Both my companions were nearby, both safe, both streaking for home. "Beaver Red, I'm showing 'E' on fuel," said Mendoza, Heming's wingman.

"Lean your mixture," said Heming. "We can coast straight in. How's your fuel, Park?"

"Needle's still wiggling," I said. "How's yours?"

"I'm flying on the fumes," he answered. "But we'll make it."

We did, clearing the area with a call as we approached, then dropping behind each other to set down on the dirt at proper intervals. Heming landed and swung off. Mendoza landed, and as he turned toward the taxi lane, his engine ran dry. That was the second time he'd quit on a runway, and he would now have a reputation for it. And since he hadn't cleared the runway, he might well be the death of me. I veered abruptly to the crossing runway and twisted my plane down on that. It was very short, and I braked in a cloud of dust to keep from running off it. By the time I reached my revetment, I couldn't have had more than a teaspoon or two of fuel. John, my crew chief, told me he looked into the tanks with a flashlight and they weren't even damp.

During the wet time, I thought back to that good day when we were credited with driving off those bombers. But we hadn't been able to do much about the night attacks. We'd gotten used to the jungle's night sounds, the howls, croaks, and sudden shrill cries—mostly stilled now, as the rains continued. But even on these wet nights the Japanese bombed us quite regularly from above the clouds. We'd wake to the high-pitched beat of twin engines up there in the blackness, going flat-out with no synchronization: bombers on their run. Then we'd hear that unforgettable "whish-whish-whish-whish-WHISH-WHISH" of bombs on their way, and we'd dash out and dive for the wet slit trenches as the world turned into one quaking, thundering, crumping blast after another, mingled with the yowling of shrapnel and the crashing of great boughs falling.

When it was over, the sounds rumbling away like a summer storm, we'd check up on one another. I don't think anyone got hurt in those raids except when late wakers leapt on top of early trench seekers. Our new intelligence officer, a most likable man named Schoen, had a strong propensity to save his hide, and so earned a lot of abrasions and the nickname "Slit Trench Sam."

We all swore to dig our own slit trenches nearer our tents, and Steve, Ben, and I dug one—the deepest and best-engineered in camp. Other people came around to look at it as we kept going down into the black forest soil, shielding it from the rain with a tarpaulin, shoring it up with poles, even roofing it with sod. Everyone started copying it. Then, when it was almost finished, we woke to find it filled to the brim with water. We'd apparently struck a spring. We made do with three shallow foxholes, and left "the swimming pool," to breed mosquitoes. It may well be still there.

Heming, the only pilot qualified to fly effectively at night, volunteered to become the squadron night fighter. He went up several times during breaks in the weather, patrolling at the time when the Japanese usually came. One night he chased a bomber and took a shot, but he didn't get it. He liked this job and actually stayed pretty sober to carry it out.

I was curious about night fighting and asked Heming about it. He had accepted me since Red Flight's madcap adventure of the impromptu strafe and intercept. I'd stayed with him that time, screaming through the palm trees to blast those shacks, then looping cannon shells at the elusive Japanese bombers, and now he liked having me in his flight. Perhaps he thought I was a real killer at heart, nostrils flaring at the smell of gunsmoke. I'd found him an interesting and complex guy.

But asking him about flying was like asking someone about the most intimate sensations of sex. He couldn't put into words the details of his addiction. Flying to him was life, love, breath, glory. His feelings for it went far too deep to be easily dislodged for the curiosity of others.

The weather relented and let the C-47s through. Food at last! Even bully beef tasted great. And now our mess sergeant heard that a navy vessel had pulled into Finschafen, and he wangled a flight there, carrying along some extra bottles of whiskey. U.S. Navy vessels had real food—hell, the swabbies were gaining weight out there. They had so many preserved eggs they were sick of them. What they didn't have was booze. The AAF was the only service that issued liquor. So for the price of two bottles of rye, our mess sergeant flew back to Tsili with several cartons of eggs.

We had them for breakfast, and when the folks from the 40th Squadron heard about it and came sniffing around our mess tent like hungry jackals, we relented and let them have some, too. We'd been given powdered eggs sometimes in the past—they furnished a strange-tasting, gluey mush—but preserved or not, these eggs were the first real ones we'd seen for months.

No sooner did the weather clear than the Japanese fooled us by staging a daylight raid. I was off-duty, and since Jerry had been sent home, I was washing some moldy, stinking clothes in the shallow river. The whishing sound caught me squatting naked, in the stream. I raced ashore and flung myself down as the sound grew enormous and then the blasts walked toward me with earth-shaking steps. I gripped the grass with my hands and tried to pull myself flatter on the ground. And the explosions came closer, ringing like great bells in my head as they got too loud for my senses to handle. Trees crashed nearby, and shrapnel hummed.

I breathed the cordite and stared at a big red ant on a blade of grass six inches from my face. The blade bent, and lowered the ant to within a couple of inches, too close for my one open eye to focus on. "Don't you mess with me, you little bastard," I told the ant. "I've got trouble enough."

And the ant moved off, and so did the bombs.

Washing clothes seemed to produce small adventures. On another day off-duty I was scouring away in the river when an Australian patrol sloshed across it and headed off into the jungle—six Diggers, led by a corporal. They appeared silently, stepped across without a word, and vanished soundlessly into the bush.

Ten days later, there I was again, getting rid of fresh stinks, and here came the same patrol. They just appeared out of nowhere at the river's edge, and joyfully flung themselves down into it. They were bearded, their jungle greens mud-stained and black with sweat. The only clean things about them were their rifles, stacked on the river bank. They sat in the water and filled their slouch hats with it, and poured it over themselves, and splashed one another.

This time they grinned happily at me, and I waded across to greet them. "Only six of you?" I queried. "I thought a patrol was bigger."

The corporal smiled up at me innocently. "You know 'ow it is, mate. If we thought we'd meet a battalion of Nips, we might take as many as a dozen."

Flying now was intense. The missions to Rabaul started, and we patrolled while the '38s refueled. Guppy showed up one of those days, when Steve and I were both on patrol. He was waiting at our flight line when we landed, and we took him back to our tent and broke out a fresh bottle. He looked around at our little jungle home distastefully, and sniffed. "I didn't know there were skunks in New Guinea, or is it you two?" He said we should be ashamed living this way. We told him he should have been here when it was rough.

We asked him about the Rabaul missions. He said the sky there was black with army Tonys and navy Zekes, and that every time MacArthur made a thundering pronouncement that Rabaul was neutralized, the Japanese answered with even more fighters and even thicker ack-ack. The P-38s had done well, zapping through the whirling enemy formations the way they were supposed to, and taking few losses. Guppy had scored again. A Zeke.

"And I flew formation with one for a while," he added. "Suddenly there he was on my wing, the pilot all huddled up with helmet and goggles and oxygen mask. He looked over at me, and I looked back at him, and the bastard eased his flaps down so he could slow up and get behind me, and I did the same to stay with him. He'd have dropped his wheels, next, and I'd probably have stalled out. But some other planes came whizzing around us, and he broke away, and I did too."

Guppy said it was a funny feeling to be so close to a Japanese fighter pilot. "He looked pretty much like any of us," he said. "I wonder if he got through that day OK."

He then told the wonderful story of the Japanese pilot who had shared a ride south with him, the first time he went on leave. The guy was short, like a fighter pilot, and slender, like anyone who put in time in New Guinea. He had short black hair and sideburns, and he sat, unmoving, between two enormous Australian MPs, built like Olympic shot-putters.

Guppy sat opposite, looking at the three of them, bored to death as the C-47 droned south toward Sydney. And suddenly the Japanese pilot stretched and said to Guppy—in the accents of the University of California—"...am I glad to get out of that...mess!"

Our stupid patrols over Tsili and Nadzab were interrupted by some fine strafing missions. The Australian army asked for strikes against Japanese gun emplacements in the Finisterres, the mountain range where they'd penetrated and met entrenched Japanese troops. We'd find the target on our maps and rake it over with all guns, and try to stop at the right place—before we strafed the Diggers. Sometimes we'd see a figure leap up and wave a big hat at us, and then we'd know to stop, and we'd slow-roll over the Aussie foxholes while they climbed out to wave.

A pair of Wirraways led us on a couple of strafes. Few today remember the Wirraway, a little two-seater Aussie plane that looked like an American AT-6—now called the T-6. It also looked a bit like a Japanese Zeke, so eager Yank pilots were apt to cut loose at it. One of our guys shot a couple down—thank God the men bailed out—and became known as the Japanese ace. After that sort of thing, whenever a Wirraway met American fighters, the gunner-observer in the rear cockpit would stand up and wave frantically.

Wirraways made a name for themselves right after Pearl Harbor, when six of them comprised the total air force of Rabaul. They took on the whole Japanese invasion, and were shot down, one by one. Now they were used for spotting, and we'd follow a pair of them to some place in the hills. They'd call in a target for us and we'd do our best to pound it. Maybe we did some good. We never knew.

Rightfully discouraged about their Wirraways, the Australians began using their new Boomerangs. They'd designed this stubby little single-seater to maneuver with a Zero, but it wasn't powerful enough to compete as a fighter. For low-level ground support, however, the Boomerang was great. A pair of them could get right below tree level, and blast hidden targets.

We'd put a flight of P-39s up with them, and cover them while they ducked almost out of sight down on the deck, and then they'd call us: "Beaver, follow our tracers," and we'd see the red lines focusing on a spot, and never taking our eyes off it, we'd peel away and lay our sights on it and trigger off our guns. We could feel that we were being helpful.

Flying home with the Boomers, we'd invariably get "shot down" by them. Those Aussies were all frustrated fighter pilots, and as soon as we got near Tsili, they'd pull up in a loop and come down on our tails, and we'd squirm and wiggle to get away, and try to turn into them. No chance. That plane was unbelievably quick and supple. You'd cram around after it, and it would be inside your turn in no time, the pilot yelling in your earphones: "Ba-ba-ba-ba-ba-ba! Got you, Yank! You're bloody dead!"

Pretty humbling. We knew what it would have been like to dogfight with the Zeroes.

We got to know this army co-op squadron of the RAAF. They shared our dreadful mess with us, and we got drunk with them and they taught us a lot of new dirty songs.

One day a squadron of Australian dive-bombers arrived at Tsili-Tsili, found billets for the night, then showed up bright and early at our alert tent. They were to pull off a strike in the Finisterres, and we were to cover them. They flew Vultee Vengeances—surely ranked among the world's worst aircraft. The plane was an adult version of an American army basic trainer in widespread use by aviation cadets, the Vultee BT-13, popularly dubbed "Vultee Vibrator" or "Vultee Vomiter," depending on one's experience in it. The latter was my choice since the day in basic when I did acrobatics in one and learned firsthand that the BT-13 poured exhaust fumes into the cockpit. It was the only time I ever chucked up in an airplane.

Of course I was quick to ask one of the Aussies if the Vengeance was as awful as the Vomiter, and he assured me happily that it certainly was, and that he couldn't wait to get the bloody thing into the air and do some dive-bombing. Those guys were all hot for action that morning.

The trouble was, the weather was horrible—about a 300-foot ceiling. They took off, anyway, and we followed them and caught them on course, and we all trudged over the hills together, clinging close to the ground, while heavy clouds walled us in and pressed us down to the murky earth.

When the cloud wall blocked our course, we fighters decided we'd had it. Whoever was leading called the Vengeances and broke it gently that we couldn't cope with this kind of sky, and we'd have to abort fast in order to find our way home. The Aussies said they understood, but they'd plough on a little farther. After all, they needed no escort in this soup. The Japanese fighters couldn't cope with it, either.

We followed the terrain back toward Tsili, and it was then, as we peered down at the ground barely 100 feet below us, that some of us spotted a crocodile. It was beside a broad marsh, writhing toward the water, and though there was nothing down there to measure it against, we agreed later that it was over 20 feet long.

The Vultee Vengeances came back, wheezing and rattling, after their unescorted mission. They'd been safe enough from air attack, but they'd had to remain so low that they had little idea of where they'd been. They were frustrated at not getting their chance to win the war singlehanded, but pleased with themselves for having made the flight despite the weather. Some of them had dropped their bombs, just for the hell of it.

The Aussies didn't accuse us of chickening out of that sortie, but we felt guilty, nonetheless. So when we got orders to do some dive-bombing ourselves we knew it was retribution. The mission started, a little inauspiciously, by Guthrie calling us together and asking if anyone had ever dive-bombed.

No one had, not even Heming.

There was a pause while we solemnly kicked at clods of mud. Then Herkimer spoke up: "There was a movie about navy dive-bombers not long ago."

"Sure," said Ferguson, "Pat O'Brien and..."

"They all have Pat O'Brien in them," put in Kelvin.

"...Robert Taylor, I think," continued Ferguson, "and...was it Virginia Mayo?"

"Probably Priscilla Lane," said Canuck.

And on it went until Guthrie suggested that we shut up. "What about the movie?" he asked Herkimer.

"Well, there was a scene where you could see the target through the sight the way the pilot saw it. He lifted the sight above it by about a rad."

"But that would have been in less than a vertical dive, wouldn't it?" asked Guthrie.

"You probably would center the sight if you were vertical," said Steve.

"If we try diving vertically in '39s, we'll bore right through New Guinea," said Canuck.

"Right," said Guthrie. "We've got to make shallow dives or we'll never pull out. So where do we sight?"

In the end, we settled on lifting the sight 3 rads (radii) above the target and giving ourselves some 500 feet to mush groundward as we pull out. And so we set out, with 500-pound bombs in place of belly tanks, on perhaps the first dive-bombing mission in which the only pilot training came from a half-remembered Hollywood film.

We flew over the Finisterres and spotted a small hill that fitted the description of the target. We couldn't be absolutely sure. A red circle penciled on a topographical grid map doesn't easily relate to a rumpled carpet of green below the wing. We circled several times, looking for a stream, and at last caught a glitter under the forest canopy. "Watch me first, Beaver," came Guthrie's voice as we circled well above. Then he rocked on his side, peeling off, and down he went, a darting little drab-colored shape. We could see him get low, then pull up and away.

I never saw his bomb explode—it would have been down below the trees somewhere. But as we fell into line astern in our wide circle, I kept my eyes on the spot in the hills where he'd been aiming. It seemed to be a small, rather abrupt peak. Just what it was supposed to be.

We peeled off and down, one after the other, going "around the clock," as the navy pilots had done in that movie. When my turn came, I found myself heading down toward that little hump just as the last plane in White Flight scudded away from it at an angle to my dive. The idea was to come in from ever-varying directions and give enemy flak a hard time.

Howling down, I watched the hilltop get bigger. It seemed a little hazy, as though a small cloud was forming over it, so I guessed White Flight's bombs were going off.

It came up faster and faster. Why didn't they shoot at me? I wondered. Those enemy gunners would never get a better chance—a plane boring straight down, unwavering. No deflection needed. Just a straight shot. I kept expecting it, but it didn't come. Then I forgot flak because I knew I must be close enough. All that wondering and worrying had taken place in about six seconds.

I yanked the belly-tank release (now used as the bomb release) and pulled out. Suddenly 500 pounds lighter, the plane leapt with new life under me. We reached upward, away from the haze of warfare, up to the bright blue. And my cheeks sagged and I clenched my stomach against the blackout, the old familiar wrenching of the body back to sensibility.

I let the little plane climb, and then, with plenty of speed still on the clock, I eased it to the top of a loop, inverted, and looked downward through my canopy to see if the target was still there or had vanished by now in a blaze of flame. And of course I saw nothing. So I rolled right-side up—completing an Immelmann—and rejoined the Beavers.

We landed, exhilarated by the flying, yet all of us, I think, as disturbed as I was about the uncertainty of our mission. We'd staked 16 expensive aircraft, four tons of explosive, and, come to think of it, our lives on a mere bet that we had the right target for a kind of attack none of us had ever tried before. A pretty sloppy way to win a war.

So I still find it unbelievable to remember that a couple of days later a transport flew into Tsili and unloaded, among other things, a case of Scotch. It was addressed to our squadron from an Australian general. A note explained that it was in thanks for as nice a piece of dive-bombing as he'd seen—right on the money.

We'd cleaned out a gun position that had been holding up the Diggers, and they'd secured that hill and gone on. Clearly, those big, gaunt, tired men down there liked to see our muddy little 'Cobras with yellow noses flying over them.

We skunk-smelling Beavers of Tsili-Tsili had somehow managed to strike a tiny tap for the Free World.

CHAPTER
ELEVEN

GETTING TO KNOW
MINE ENEMY

As I look back at our Tsili-Tsili duty, it seems to have gone on for an eternity. Day after day we flew stupid patrols, interlaced with scrambles. Night after night we dove for the slit trenches. It was a one-sided war—the Japanese trying to kill us every night, we serenely buzzing around the sky every day, not even breaking the tape on our gun muzzles. Our frustration was one reason so many of us went bonkers when a Japanese soldier wandered into our camp.

First, our squadron cooks began noticing unexplainable gaps in our meager food supplies. Then someone spotted a figure in the night, slinking away from our kitchen area. And finally, one of our aviation mechanics rose from his sack to relieve himself early in the morning, and saw the man himself—short, stocky, stealthy, scared, and unmistakably Japanese.

Beaver Squadron reacted by plunging into hopeless chaos. Air raids we could cope with. But we had no experience with a ground attack, and even though it consisted of one lost Japanese army grunt scrounging for food, our ground troops contemplated the invasion with a mixture of panic and fascination. The rumor mill whirred: This was an advance scout for a regiment of picked commando-type jungle fighters who had been ordered to wipe Tsili-Tsili off the map. Wrong. This was no scout, but one of the main body—already in place for a screaming banzai charge this very night!

Even we pilots—at first highly amused by the situation— began to suffer moments of wild conjecture. Our expensive

113

and meticulous training hadn't included ground warfare. We felt as helpless as would a company of infantry, suddenly faced with scrambling to Angels Twenty in our Airacobras. Following the sighting, four or five of the pilots began wearing their Colts on their hips instead of leaving them hanging on a nail to gather rust, as we all normally did when off-duty.

As for the ground personnel—mechanics, armorers, radio technicians, clerks, cooks, drivers, and medics—they stormed into the armament tent and began wandering around with pistols, bayonets, and those nice little carbines we'd tried hunting wild pigs with. The supply officer, obviously a fire eater at heart, showed up at lunch that first Day of the Alien with a pair of Colts, a carbine strapped on his back, and an Australian Sten gun hanging from one shoulder. "How about a cavalry saber?" Steve asked.

"For every rat you see, there's a hundred you don't see," he muttered ominously.

Of course the benighted enemy was doomed. Someone, a sentry I think, shot him that evening. The supply officer never had a chance to pull one of those four triggers and had to put his spectacles back on and return to the dull world of inventories.

But he did satisfy some gruesome urge by taking a flash picture of the corpse. He showed it around, later, when we'd all forgotten the incident. The enemy's face was broad and pasty white, an ugly peasant face in a body considerably fatter than any of ours. The poor, dumb bastard had obviously been a slave to his stomach. He could have made it to his own people if he'd had willpower enough to go hungry. His own gluttony killed him as much as the surprising bloodthirst of our hitherto peaceful and hardworking ground staff.

Not long after that small excitement we saw more enemies. They were two prisoners cooped in an outdoor cage at the big new base that had been scraped out of the tall grass of Nadzab. There, in the broad valley of the Markham River, now free of paratroopers and crowded with engineers building new airstrips. We were finally ordered to relocate. Good-by to the jungle and its skunk bugs. Farewell to days of hunger, to the loneliness of our wilderness sidetrack, of feeling that our destiny had been stacked on a dusty War Department shelf and there forgotten. Suddenly we were landing at Nadzab on a shiny new strip of steel matting, setting up camp, contemplating new missions with more to do, and now taking our first closeup look at live foemen.

Only two enemies, actually. One was a sick and skinny lad who clutched at the wire fencing and kept repeating, in garbled English, that he was a Korean. That was undoubtedly true, since the Japanese had pressed Koreans into hard labor, and they were quick to surrender if they ever had a chance.

But the second POW was a prototype Japanese. He sat in the middle of the corral, as far from the wire walls as he could get. He was a husky man, medium height, strongly built, close-cropped black hair with sideburns, black eyes fixed on some distant point, never deigning to glance at the troops outside who peered in at him. He wore shorts and a torn military shirt of faded khaki, and he sat impassively, hands clasped around his knees, never saying a word, never changing expression.

Men tossed a cigarette or two to the Korean, and he grinned and chattered and begged for more. Someone had thrown one to the Japanese. It lay on the ground beside him, untouched.

I suppose that soldier had been taken at Lae when it fell to the Aussies shortly before our move to Nadzab. Soon after our arrival, three of us, off-duty, cadged a jeep and headed east on the track to Lae. It was natural, I think, to want to visit what had for so long been such a formidable enemy base. But the drive to it was an unexpected adventure. Even the word "track" was an exaggeration for the little trace through the rain forest that we followed. We made full use of the jeep's built-in winch, hauling ourselves out of bottomless mudholes. Even so, we had to give up at one point and gratefully allow an Australian weapons carrier to wrench us out of a gluey crevasse.

(Years later, I made the same drive effortlessly and looked back on that mud-spattered expedition of 1943. Now I was on a partially surfaced highway, and every car I met was Japanese. My rented sedan was a Toyota.)

Our primitive trail finally emerged at the Lae airstrip. An Australian work party was busy patching its bomb craters, bulldozing wrecked planes to the side. We stared in wonder at the lifeless pieces of junk with those awesome red circles on their crumpled wings. We investigated twin-barreled ack-ack guns, beautifully made to pump explosive shells at P-39s.

A great pile of clothing near the end of the strip drew our attention, and we approached it gingerly, since the whole place stank, and we didn't feel like running across rotten bodies. But the smell was more of filth than of death—the stench, I suppose, of utter defeat—and the heap of clothes, ready for burning, revealed interesting things. We all indulged in a little scavenging.

I thought it might be pretty cool (an expression we didn't use, back then) to wear a Japanese shirt, and I chose one that looked my size. Also jungle-green pants and a pair of sneakers with the big toe separated. Then I spotted a well-made wooden rice chest with Japanese stenciling and rope handles. I used it to carry my newly filched clothing.

As we were gladly leaving that desolate hill of enemy belongings, we noticed a number of women's dresses and brightly colored kimonos. We'd heard rumors about the Japanese supplying prostitutes for their troops. Now we saw evidence. We also saw a towel. On it, in red letters were English words: "U.S. MARINES." And under that: "WAKE ISLAND."

Heading back toward our jeep, we passed a Digger going through a pile of equipment. "Want a rifle, mate?" he called. We walked over. He showed us at least a dozen Japanese infantry rifles, still smeared with cosmoline from the factory. They'd never been fired.

But we had no room, and the Aussie simply shrugged and walked on. Then I saw something white on the ground and picked up a 6-foot-long "scarf of a thousand stitches," the band that Japanese pilots often wore around their heads or bodies. The stitches, each added by a different relative, depicted the rising sun and its rays, and the scarf was supposed to bring luck. But this sun had been desecrated by a bullet hole right through the center, surrounded by a smear of blood.

It seemed that though every item of our booty proclaimed our triumph, it also attested to the utter, hopeless debasement of human beings in defeat. We left Lae curiously dispirited by the spoils of victory.

Back in our own camp, I tried to get a Papuan laundry boy—not another Jerry, unfortunately—to wash my captured clothing. He wouldn't. He said they smelled of the Japanese and would make all the other clothes smell that way too. I washed them myself, and tried them on. The shirt smelled bad to me, too, and the pants were too small. I threw them both away. The split-toed sneakers gave me horrendous blisters, and I gave them to another guy, and eventually he threw them away.

I still have the scarf of a thousand stitches. At first sight of it my wife washed it thoroughly. But the bloodstain is still there, a faint smudge beside the bullet hole. The rice box is beside me in my studio as I write. The rope handles have rotted away, but otherwise it's in fine shape. It's filled with story ideas that never came to anything, with articles that were never finished or that were rejected and not yet rewritten. It's a fine box, but it still seems to be full of defeat.

Our first camp at Nadzab was wet as well as hot and uncomfortable, and we shifted to a drier site out in the kunai. The sun's heat here was so intense that we were forced to be ingenious, scrounging lumber when we could to floor our tents and cutting away the grass—sometimes eight feet tall—to allow air to circulate.

Our sudden visibility made us a prime bombing target, but we remembered how seldom the Japanese had come over us in daylight back at Tsili-Tsili. We'd be OK, we told one another. Hell, it was worth a little danger to be a little cooler. We went about making life as comfortable as possible.

Steve, Ben Briker, and I cadged a small supply parachute, left over from the building of the Tsili-Tsili base, and spread it out inside our pyramidal tent to give us a false ceiling under the blistering hot oiled canvas. The insulating effect was the envy of other tents, and since there were few of these little 'chutes, those of us who got one felt we had to rationalize our right to it: We were in an especially hot area; we were subject to severe heat rash; we thought of the idea first.

Strangely, the rest of the squadron gave us little flak about our small luxury. We realized that we'd been in the squadron for a long time now, and were regarded as important—if somewhat senile—elders. Even I, whose mastery of the fighter pilot role had always been tentative, found myself flying with new relish.

The fact was that flying with Heming made me aware that I did indeed have a certain capacity for recklessness and could, it seemed, turn it on at will. And of course that's exactly what a *real* fighter pilot must have, even today.

The base at Nadzab grew apace. Sheets of steel matting were pinioned together on every cleared patch of kunai, and strip after strip appeared, some 14 in all. New squadrons appeared, entire new groups, fresh from the States. There were B-25s everywhere. Those mediums had proved themselves, and General Kenney wanted more. And now new fighters came, huge but graceful P-47s—Thunderbolts, or, as their pilots called them, "Jugs."

Campsites sprouted all over the valley. A field hospital was established. One of the Mayos from the famous clinic in Minnesota ran it. A couple of movie screens appeared, one not far from our camp, and night after night, until the air raid guns went off, we'd go to see Hollywood's wartime efforts.

We watched a lot of war films, including flying stories in which Van Johnson or some other unlikely fighter pilot battled a Japanese pilot in evil-looking goggles who flew a Zero which we quickly recognized as the good old AT-6 that we'd all trained on. The enemy pilot would hiss through his big teeth, "Die, you Yankee dog!" And then Van Johnson would get a burst in, and the Japanese pilot would slump forward with a rush of black stuff from his mouth, and the AT-6 would tilt forward on the screen, and apparently dive straight into the

ground with horrendous sound effects. Van would miraculous-
ly be sent home to the loving arms of Priscilla Lane or someone, and the film would always end with a shot of the
American flag flapping bravely.

They say wandering Japanese soldiers would sometimes
watch those films, standing in the rear, unnoticed. I guess
they thought them pretty funny, too.

We had proof that the Japanese infiltrated us on the
ground. It would have been harder to do that in the air, but
Doug Horachov and I saw it happen once. We'd just landed at
our Nadzab strip after escorting a squadron of C-47s to the
mountain strip that we called Bena Bena. It served Garoka,
where we had a new fighter sector with radar. We had beaten
the big transports home and were walking back to the alert
tent when they circled their strip to land. We stopped to watch
them, all olive drab, all rumbling around the pattern.

"Hey," said Doug, "how come there are thirteen of them?"

I counted:…ten, eleven, twelve, thirteen. Everybody knew
a transport squadron was twelve planes. "They must have an
extra," I said.

And then the last plane in the circuit peeled away and
headed off to the north, to Japanese country. Maybe Doug and
I showed up—very small—in the photos that the people in
that thirteenth plane had been taking of Nadzab.

We Beavers flew a great deal—two, sometimes three missions a day—because Nadzab was the perfect springboard for
patrols over the Markham and Ramu valleys and above the
Finisterres where the Australians were doing their stuff. We
strafed a great deal. We escorted B-25s—a job we liked because
they were fast and sure, thundering in very low, blasting everything in sight, then gone like a flash, and we with them.

One day we had to escort a Catalina on a rescue mission
off the north coast. This was the navy's great old PBY amphib-
ian, called the "Cat" by everyone. It was used for patrols and
to pick up downed pilots as they floated in their little rubber
rafts. Some units, Australian as well as American, painted
their Cats black and used them for night bombing at Rabaul.

The story goes that one "Black Cat" squadron would drop nuisance bombs, fuses timed to set them off at intervals so the Japanese couldn't sleep. When their bomb racks were empty, they'd tie three empty beer bottles together at the necks and spin them out of their gun ports so they'd scream all the way down. A fiendish, banshee wail getting louder and louder, followed by a small tinkle. Talk about psychological warfare!

On our rescue mission, the old navy Cat lumbered along, low and slow, while our two flights fussed and fidgeted 5000 feet above it, weaving back and forth like sheep dogs with a lame ewe. Sometimes one flight would chase off to investigate some distant spot in the sky or a tree-shrouded cove along the shore where enemy supply barges might hide. Then we'd be back in a flash, all filled with impatience and excitement about what the Cat would find and how it would react.

We continued farther along the coast, well into enemy country, now deeply committed to this mission. If a Japanese fighter patrol spotted that Cat, we were in for the fight of our lives. If one of our engines failed—always a consideration in a P-39—we'd be down in an enemy-controlled patch of sea, but at least with a good chance to be rescued by the big, awkward beast we'd been shepherding. I remember my eyes burning from their endless search of the sky in every direction, my seat numb from sitting for so long on what seemed a slab of granite: parachute and folded dinghy.

Oddly, I can't remember exactly how the mission turned out. I know the Cat landed beside a tiny island. We were so busy trying to spot the attacking Zeroes which we *knew* must be on the way that we could only spare glances to make sure we were orbiting on station. None of us saw our Cat's black rubber dinghy move ashore or return. We knew that only after giving the enemy a seemingly endless opportunity to storm onto the scene and clobber us all, we saw the wake of the Cat taking off, and renewed our protective weaving, but this time moving gradually back toward home and safety.

For our own security, we kept radio silence in the air, but after landing, we beseiged Slit Trench Sam to tell us the outcome of that mission. But communication with the navy was sporadic, and Sam never heard from those people. Was the downed pilot found alive and rescued? Was his body discovered, torn by bullets or, as was sometimes the case, beheaded? Was he ever found at all? We never knew.

We also wondered why we weren't attacked during so vulnerable a flight. The Japanese would have caught us cold-cock if they'd come down on us out of the sun. How could they resist the pleasure of clobbering eight war-weary Airacobras? Were their supply lines now too fragile for them to face a single loss? Back when our squadron arrived in New Guinea, in 1942, our planes were at first ordered out to sea during Japanese raids on Moresby. Only when more planes and pilots arrived could we risk a few. Were the Japanese now in the same boat? Were we finally winning? Would Washington now finally have a moment to spare for this forsaken squadron? How about new planes? Food supplies, hmm? Rotation home?

Flushed with novel notions of victory, we scoffed at our enemy and loudly hoped we'd get one or two before they pulled up stakes and fled New Guinea. And then one morning, as we choked down the usual breakfast of "French toast and bacon," the damned enemy strafed us.

Ben and I were both off-duty that day, so we'd slept late and slid into the officers' table just in time to get the last slices of cold, stale bread, soggy with warm, sweetened water, and the last slabs of slimy, half-cooked pork fat. We were eyeing it with resignation and skimming away the red ants that popped up in our sugared coffee, when we became aware of a new, intrusive sound amid the usual rumble of aircraft engines revving up in preflight. It was a distant rattle that quickly increased in volume along with the now familiar high-pitched yowl of a Japanese engine with throttle and rpms slammed fully forward.

In a half-second, the mess tent's friendly, morning hum of voices went silent. In the next half second, everyone who had been seated at the long tables was under them. Ben and I bumped heads as we dove together. Huddled under the wood planking—through which a bullet could pass without slowing up—we apologized gravely to each other. "At least, there goes breakfast," I said.

"I certainly hope so," he agreed.

The strafing plane swept past, above the canvas roof, and amid shouts of "Watch out for his wingman!" everyone erupted from the tent. No one seemed to want to be caught dead beside French toast and bacon.

Ben and I now had rank enough to sometimes corral a jeep. We did so, quickly, and headed toward the flight line with the idea that there'd be a scramble, and if the duty pilots had taken casualties from the strafing we might be needed. Dink Cahill yelled at us to wait, and we slowed as he jumped for the back seat. Trust Dink. If there was any chance for action, he was there.

I was driving. I slid around a corner onto the road that flanked our airstrip and led to our flight line. And as soon as I straightened out on it, I found myself staring at a plane coming at me fast and low, spots of bright light winking from its wings.

Wordlessly, I slammed on the brakes and we all dove under the jeep. Again I banged my head on something, but didn't really feel it until that evening. Harsh sounds lashed us—the crack and whine of bullets hitting and ricocheting, and behind all, the almost falsetto scream of that Japanese engine, approaching, then abruptly changing key in Doppler effect as the plane whipped overhead.

Warily we emerged to see if he was going to make another pass. But heavy ground machine guns were now hammering at him, and we watched him climb and peel off northward, back to *his* barn. We didn't see his wingman, though we knew that two planes, probably those fast, sharp-nosed Tonys, pulled off the attack.

Hot, dirty, and bruised, the three of us got back in the jeep. The engine started perfectly, the gears worked, the tires were hard and round. But as we continued toward our flight line, I found I was staring at a small round hole in the windscreen, directly in front of me. Wordlessly, I pointed it out to the others.

"Hell, Park," said Ben. "He was after you."

"Son of a bitch was a pretty good shot too," added Dink. "That would have gone right between your eyes. What a mess to clean up!"

"For you," I said. "Not for me."

Our colleagues on flight duty, including Steve, were angry and embarrassed. The early patrol—two flights—hadn't been long off the ground when the strafers came. The other two flights got no warning. "Just a bunch of bullets flying around," said Steve. They never had a hope of intercepting.

Nothing much was hit, fortunately none of our people. But the attack had its effects. We felt stupidly vulnerable, and tried to improve our defenses. Slit trenches appeared beside every tent and several beside gathering places like the mess tent and alert tent. Revetments for parked aircraft were spread out and their sides beefed up for better protection.

The fighter squadrons, sprouting like mushrooms around this broad valley, began to scramble after everything in the air—birds, clouds, raindrops, Australian and American medium bombers, and each other. Sure, we had our radio identification signal, called IFF, which constantly showed our position to the sector, but gosh, maybe those tricky, untrustworthy Japanese had that system figured out.

The story of Pinky Squadron calling in a Japanese flight made its rounds. Pinky was a great old outfit, one of the earliest American fighter squadrons to reach New Guinea, and its P-40s did a lot of work. And one day, as the squadron was stooging along on patrol, every earphone in Pinky erupted: "Pinky Leader from Pinky Blue Two; bandits, ten o'clock high!" And: "Pinky from Pinky White Four; bandits, ten high, ten high!" And then: "This is Pinky Leader. I see them. I see them." And then a new voice: "We see you too, Pinky."

Every measly aviation cadet had to study aircraft identification, and it was well taught with accurate silhouette models. But those classrooms were vastly different from the boiling tropical clouds at 15,000 feet, when eyesight was tempered by anxiety and weariness, by sector's assurance that the bandits were *right there,* and by the rush of adrenalin when a distant glimpse actually showed an aircraft.

If it was a Wirraway, watch out! Australian Beauforts, too, had to be careful. They looked a lot like some of the Japanese light bombers. So did the American A-20. So, especially, did the big, fast Martin B-26, a near twin of the Japanese Betty bomber.

We Beavers were scrambled one afternoon and sent over the hills northwest of Nadzab. Sector assured us that we had a solid target, a steadily moving flight of planes, in formation, with no IFF to identify them. "Vector two-nine-five to Charlie Eight. You should meet them at Angels Thirteen."

We followed 295 degrees and came into the coordinates C-8 on our little grid maps at precisely 13,000 feet. And by God, there was a flight of 12 silver bombers in Japanese formation—a vee of vees—headed hell-bent for Nadzab! We didn't even call them in for fear they'd be tuned to our frequency as those Zeroes had been to Pinky's. We just nodded our helmeted heads at one another, edged upward to get between them and the sun, and then spread out a little so that everyone had a clean shot.

And down we came, gunsights on, gun switches on, every hand on the belly-tank release. Flying Red Three, I got a bomber in my sight, growing larger quickly—twin engines, the high rudder of a Betty. I eased my finger onto the trigger that prodded from my control stick. Only one hit from my 37-millimeter cannon would blow this bastard to bits. I thought of the Betty that had clobbered me on my first combat. I wasn't green any more, and this was *my* turn.

And then the unbelievable: White stars showed up on wingtips and fuselages. Everyone saw them at once. Our squadron leader didn't have to say "Don't shoot." He just peeled away, and we all banked with him, and the leader of that crack B-26 squadron—they called themselves "The Great Silver Fleet," after an airline back home—jauntily wagged his wings to greet us.

He'd led his bomber boys on a long, hairy mission, shutting off his IFF because those incredibly Machiavellian Japanese would likely be tuned in to it. And—oops!—he'd forgotten to turn it back on. But no harm done, right? And it sure felt good to see a squadron of friendly fighters slide up alongside!

C H A P T E R
T W E L V E

THE RESORT
HOTEL

My next leave seemed a long time coming, and like the "young fighter pilot" of our song, "with blood on his tunic and mud on his knees," I almost crawled down to Sydney. Three missions a day had taken their toll on all of us. We had stepped from our planes after each flight and invariably remarked, "God, I'm tired." And Kelvin used to answer, "Glad to meet you, Tired. But my name's Kelvin." And we'd giggle helplessly.

We weary Beavers now knew one another so well that conversation among us became an argot of private sayings and jokes that short-circuited logical lines of communication. After landing from a strafing mission or a scramble, we'd trudge into the alert tent to collapse until the next flight—a patrol, perhaps, or another scramble. Sam would meet us for debriefing: Had we seen anything unusual? Did we get ground fire? Any problems with the planes?

"I caught Park's prop wash and almost flipped, right over the trees," Mendoza might say after a strafe. And someone would remark, "And there I was..." and get a perfunctory laugh. The gag was, "And there I was on my back, with nothing on but the radio," but we were too tired to say all that. And now we no longer needed to.

Our special language was often silly, but sometimes pretty good. I don't know if it was in general use, but judging by the bewilderment I provoked when I "talked Air Force" back in the States, I guess not. It wasn't just that strange use of "soiree," or the more common "augering in" and "buying it." It was a special zing—often vulgar—in our talk. Herkimer returned from a soiree one day, bitterly swearing that his guns "didn't fire Round One."

Big Joe Sheehan, the armament officer, stared at him unbelieving. "You mean they quit on you?"

"That's damned straight," said Herk (or something to that effect).

The newer kids, now beginning to come out and replace the oldsters, were generally pretty innocent and nicely brought up—a far cry from the tough old boys who greeted my group of replacements. Those old pros had been Air Corps before Pearl, Depression victims, good enough to get this job of flying and keep it despite bone-deep cuts in the armed forces. They sometimes had trouble joining polite company, down on leave, and consequently didn't seek it. But the replacements, the GI pilots, could quickly spot a "back home" situation, drop their argot, and turn in a flash into charming, bright-eyed, well-spoken mama's boys.

When Ben Briker finally got sent home, he noted Steve's and my home addresses and called on our parents. "What a nice boy Ben is," wrote my mother. I thought of skinny, smelly, scrofulous, foul-mouthed, funny old Ben and smiled. So *that's* what he was, way down deep—a nice boy. Of course!

All this goes to say that leave was very welcome when it finally came. In Sydney, I found myself veering away from the frantic, boozy parties and thinking about other things I'd like to do, as far away from uniforms and shop talk about missions as I could get. Then I ran into Guppy, down from his squadron with Don Peterson. Guppie had wisdom tooth trouble. The older pilots were all at wisdom tooth age, and army dentistry was part of our lives. But Guppy's tooth had become infected, and he had to treat it with the magical new sulfa drugs before he could have it out.

So when I suggested that we team up and go to the Blue Mountains to see a little more of Australia than Sydney, he was in the mood to take me up on it. "You'll have to treat my tooth, though," he said. "Peterson's been doing it in our flat. Twice a day."

I agreed. And a day later, after a pleasant train trip, we were at a village in the hills, booked into a proper resort hotel filled with proper civilians. They'd spent a lot of money to get away from the Yanks, and they could hardly be blamed for looking at the two of us as though we were an outbreak of pregnancy in a girls' boarding school.

Guppy and I determined to behave with utmost discretion, just like everyone else. We would act as though going to a resort hotel in the Blue Mountains was something we'd done since childhood and would do for the rest of our lives. We discarded our leather flight jackets and dressed discreetly in neatly pressed uniforms with neckties. We spoke to the staff in discreetly quiet voices. We strenuously avoided staring at other guests, looking discreetly past them, even though among them were two attractive girls.

As we were entering the lobby after a sightseeing walk, Guppy remembered that it was time to treat his tooth. "What do I do?" I asked, discreetly.

"I'll show you, upstairs."

We went up to our room and he got beside a window and opened his mouth wide. "Eye eeah," he said, probing with a finger toward a nasty-looking red place.

"Got it," I said.

He closed his mouth and sat on the bed. "I have to lie down and put my head back," he said. "Peterson found that was the only way to get at the thing."

He lay down and gaped again while I got some of the sulfa on a little flat slat of wood unwrapped from a sterile packet. I showed it to him.

"Oh aih," he said.

Getting the stuff into the right spot without spilling it was tricky. Finally, by twisting his head, straddling his body, and bending close to that open mouth, I managed to aim the thing correctly and dumped its load in place, tamping it down as I'd been told.

Just then the door opened and in came a housekeeper on an inventory expedition. I jerked around. Some of the sulfa went down Guppy's throat. "Damn" he remarked, and began coughing.

"I beg your pardon," the housekeeper murmured, and vanished, obviously convinced that she had stumbled upon some unspeakable perversion—just what one might expect of those dreadful Americans.

We finished our operation in peace, and realizing that dinner would soon be served, went discreetly downstairs to the guests' lounge. Though everyone was there, the room was silent. Families spoke together in whispers, quick to hush children who forgot themselves and asked unthinkable questions like "When is tea, Mummy?" Though we tiptoed in, everyone stared at us with apparent hostility. We wondered if the housekeeper had been by to warn them about us.

We found a corner where we could sit. We could also look at the two girls, very discreetly, of course. We joined in the general silence as the clock ticked slowly toward dinner.

Then the door to the pub opened abruptly and in reeled a drunken American sergeant. He paused, swaying on his feet and staring about him in astonishment.

"Whaddsa hellsa matter?" he asked with loud cheerfulness. "Did someone die?"

There was a faintly audible gasp from all the discreet people, and a small groan from the two of us.

"Should we...?" murmured Guppy.

"He's AAF," I whispered. "I guess we have to."

If the drunk had been navy or marine corps, or another branch of the army, we'd have been able to leave him alone and simply disown him. But he wore the little winged propeller of the Army Air Forces, so he was ours. In front of everyone, we walked over to him with friendly smiles. "How'rya doing, sergeant?"

He beamed at us. "Hey, sirs! Down from the island? How about a drink?"

And the three of us vanished into the bar.

Thanks to the sergeant, we met the girls. They greeted us with inviting smiles when we returned to eat, and when we introduced ourselves they let us in on the great secret of that hotel—that every one of the guests was bored to tears with being discreet. The sight of two American pilots had indeed been a shock, said the girls, but had also raised hopes for a little excitement. A lot of the guests seemed to think that the intrusion of the sergeant was the most hilarious thing that had ever happened in that bloody place. He, and our embarrassed reaction, had cheered everyone up.

The girls said they'd about had it, up in the country, and were headed back to town next day. We went out together that evening, but there wasn't much to do. Next day Guppy and I saw the girls off—after getting their phone numbers—and then did a nature walk along the steep hills until we realized that trudging through the bush wasn't exactly new to us. We had a last great dinner that evening (the food was fine), made friends with some of the little kids in the lounge, and arranged to check out in the morning.

Back in Sydney, we found room in Guppy's squadron flat, rang the girls, and lined up a romantic evening starting with dinner at a French restaurant. The girls arrived. They were charming. They were beautiful. They wore their hair clewed up forward and streaming aft, like Rita Hayworth, and like every other attractive girl in the world in 1943. They smelled great. We went to dinner, then returned to the flat to put on some records—soft and slow.

Just as hopes for a pleasant liaison were running high, so too were my insides. I had eaten some of *le lapin* for dinner, and now had a case of le ptomaine poisoning. Guppy had to bid the girls a hasty farewell and get me into a hospital.

So the only thing we accomplished on that leave was to see the Blue Mountains, add a little zest to a tiresome old hotel, and get a fancy Sydney restaurant closed by the health department for serving tainted rabbit to a skinny American.

CHAPTER
THIRTEEN

BOMBS ALONG
THE MARKHAM

Home again among the Beavers, I went straight back to work, now occasionally leading a mission. We went, for example, on a barge hunt up the north coast of the island, where the enemy slipped at night into tiny coves and inlets, curtained by drooping palm trees. The idea was for Red Flight to search, getting low enough to look under the palms, while White Flight's four planes flew cover, hanging a little behind at about 4000 feet.

"Avoid Uligan Harbour," said Slit Trench Sam, briefing us. "Lots of antiaircraft in there."

As Red Flight leader, I headed up the mission, skimming the flat, tropical sea so close to shore that my left wing seemed about to brush the palm fronds. I peered under them at patches of still water, black in the dense shade. Any structure was Japanese. Any heap of dead fronds was camouflage for a small supply barge. Even if we in Red Flight only thought we saw something, we reported it, and swung up and away to come back in a strafing run.

We poked and searched and swooped and shot, never higher than 50 feet, the coast rushing past us, a wingspan away. Low, fast, beautiful, a delightful mission, whether or not it advanced by a centimeter the cause of virtue. And, inevitably, we had to pay for it. Concentrating on the demands of flying on the deck, where any small lapse could dump a plane into the drink, I found myself following the coastline into a neat, square-shaped indentation. And as soon as I turned the corner, the entire shoreline erupted in a blaze of flashing gun muzzles. The clear air was suddenly blackened with bursting shells.

This was the thing we all hated—ack-ack. We weren't trained to cope with it, and seldom met it. The Japanese, with their long, vulnerable supply lines, saved ammunition by opening fire only when they were dead sure of their target's range and speed. An attack by Zeroes was a familiar, almost friendly event compared with that sudden, carefully aimed Japanese flak.

"Ack-ack!" I yelled needlessly into my mike, and in a split second all eight planes were all over the sky, jinking, wheeling, spiraling, and getting out of there.

Then there was a crack like the sound of a lightning strike in the backyard, and my plane slewed to one side as though a giant had petulantly shoved it. I was sure I'd been hit. I craned to check for damage on my tail section, but could make out no torn surfaces. The controls worked perfectly.

Never one to play the hero, I called the others as soon as we were clear of the inlet. "Beaver from Red One. I think I took a hit. Red Two please check my tail section for damage."

My wingman slid in close and looked me over carefully. "Can't see anything," he said.

"You're not hurt, are you?" came Dink's voice. He was leading White Flight.

"I'm fine, but we're heading for the barn." After all, the mission was accomplished; we'd reached the return point, determined by our fuel supply.

I led the flights around and we flew back, White Flight down on the deck, this time, hoping to spot targets we'd missed. I took Red Flight upstairs, to peer now at the sky instead of those hidden inlets. My plane felt fine. But it was good to have room to bail out if it came to that.

We hummed serenely down the coast to the spot where we turned inland to avoid the guns of Madang. Leading the mission, I was responsible for knowing the way home—the course and the coordinates where I changed it. But having flown over the area so often, we all navigated by almost imperceptible guideposts as familiar as landmarks back home—the dead birch tree where you turn left, the culvert at the bottom of the hill, the rock ledge that crosses the driveway.

Here, we came to know a high bluff, yellow with kunai, where you turned inland and swept right over an almost intact Zero that had crash-landed months before. A Zeke, in fine shape, camouflaged bright green and yellow. New pilots always asked to try their guns on it, but oldsters liked it as a landmark, and some of us hoped that it might someday end up in a museum. Maybe it did.

Beyond that headland was the pass. There were dozens of passes through the Finisterres, but this one had a special shape, and we all knew it. Through the pass lay the Ramu Valley, and we'd follow it upstream, past the tiny emergency strip of Dumpu, then over the marshy land to the broad Markham Valley, and home.

At Nadzab, we barge hunters landed and taxied to our revetments. I unplugged radio and oxygen, unlatched the Sutton harness and parachute straps, peeled off helmet and goggles, and stepped out on the wing. John in his greasy shorts, baseball cap, and mahogany tan was there to help me down, a procedure he'd followed since that time—so very long ago—when my plane had been shot up.

I felt the ground under my feet again, good old planet Earth, and the sun hitting my flight suit, black with sweat, so that the moisture steamed. The tapes were gone from the gun muzzles, as they always seemed to be, these days. When I was a new Beaver, we'd recognize the special whistle our planes made when they flew back with their tapes gone, and we'd pile out to the strip to see what had happened. Were the belly tanks gone? What planes were missing?

Now we heard that whistle every time a flight landed. For every day we broke the tapes, strafing. The war was changing. The 'Cobras were being used as they were designed, doing the job for which they were built. And I liked it. Low-level work may have been demanding and hot, but it was exciting and a bit daring, without the terrible challenge of one mediocre pilot battling another, who might not be at all mediocre, high in the sky with no place to hide.

I remembered with a start that low-level work did have its dangers. "I think I got hit by ack-ack," I told John. "See anything?"

"Not a thing. Engine OK?"

"Smooth as silk. Let's look at the tail. It felt like the tail."

We scoured every inch. Not a mark. I unzipped my flight suit, rolled it down around my waist and wrapped it there, letting the sun bite into my bare shoulders. Then I got into my jeep—as today's leader I had my own jeep—and chugged off to the alert tent.

Herkimer came out to meet me, grinning broadly. "Dink told us about it," he said. "Welcome to the Uligan Harbour Skeet Club."

"You too?"

"Last week. I wandered right in there, fat, dumb, and happy, just like you. Hell! I never saw such ack-ack! Did your plane get hit?"

"Can't find a mark on it," I said. "But it felt like someone hitting my rudder with a baseball bat."

"Could you hear the bang?"

"You bet."

"Then you got a real close one, Bub."

We walked into the tent and Slit Trench Sam appeared, his face wrinkled in smiles. I switched gears to talk ground talk with him instead of air talk with Herkimer.

"Now let's see, Ted," he said, sounding like a mother whose little boy has had a problem at school. "You crossed the coast about here?"

"This little point. It's a high bluff."

"And did you cover all these inlets up to Uligan Harbour?"

"I'm pretty sure we got them all. But they're hard to see when you're low. The trees hide them."

"Trees? Can't you see the stream through the trees?"

"We're too low. We have to look under the trees."

"*Under* the trees? You can't get *that* low, can you?"

"Mostly we can. Eight feet's about low enough."

"*Eight feet!* Good God." And so on.

I got a rest, then, lying flat on a cot. But as soon as the clouds began to build over the mountains, we were scrambled, and I roared off, wondering vaguely if I really hadn't been hit at all, or if I'd find out about it any time now.

We wrenched ourselves up to 15,000 feet, and then were called back. My plane was acting perfectly, and coming down, I led my flight into a steep vertical bank and held it, so we spiraled down together, falling on our lower wings, turning fast and tight, with wingtip streamers etching corkscrews of condensation behind every plane. I knew I was close to a stall—a high-speed stall, as we called it. This resulted from such a tight turn that the wings simply lost the flow of air over them and consequently their lift. A plane would then snap-roll, and drop. If it happened to me, now, I'd instantly tumble into the jungle with no time to regain control. "Poor old Park finally augered in," the Beavers would say, I hope in regretful tones.

Was I really about to lose the bite of the air in this spiral? I held the stick with my middle finger alone, and I could feel the plane tremble against my fingertip. A tiny movement in that one finger would stall me, and I'd buy it. The difference between life and death was down to an imperceptible twitch. A tic. I contemplated it....

No. Not death yet. Not ready for it, yet. Perhaps later. With a little sigh, I eased my finger and the plane took on a solid feeling as the turn softened. We all pulled out gracefully, and thundered over the strip, stirring a cyclone of dust, and then creamed the air with our pullouts. I was nearly inverted when my wheels popped and the flaps dug the air to brake my fall. The engine gurgled and gasped in idle, and as I bent the plane onto its landing leg, still in a steep bank, I cleared its throat with a touch of throttle. Then my left wheel kissed the steel matting, the right gently followed, and I held the stick back, keeping the nose up, slowing the plane...slower...slower...until the nose wheel eased down just in time for me to turn off at the first exit.

Taxiing in, I realized that I was flying pretty well—as though the wings were part of me. I had never thought I would feel that way.

The scrambles were seldom the real thing. But sometimes the enemy came. He pulled a daring fighter sweep over

Nadzab and all the duty pilots went howling up after them. Our '39s got off, but couldn't get high enough fast enough to tangle with the Tonys. Some of the P-38 boys spotted one Tony with the nose section all painted up with little American flags. "Must have been thirty of 'em," said one pilot.

So we faced a big-time Japanese ace, and I hoped fervently I'd never meet him in a P-39 and become another flag on his cowling. But one hot-shot Lightning pilot, with 20 or so kills to his credit, swore he'd get the enemy ace and asked everyone to give him a chance at him. Of course you really couldn't hold back from combat, but this guy thought asking for it sounded good. Sort of like the World War I days.

Anyway, they did meet, right over Nadzab, and chased each other around and then disappeared in a cloud. People on the ground heard that faraway rattle of gunfire, and then one plane emerged and flew home—northward—and we never saw the hot-shot again.

Nadzab grew bigger and got more civilized. The food improved a little, and the movies got better. A traveling show from Hollywood finally came by with a girl singer who was interested only in the biggest brass on the base. She drove around in command cars with little flags snapping from their fenders, and after the two shows that were put on for us ("I just want all you wonderful boys to know that you're absolutely the most wonderful audience any of us has ever seen"), she vanished with some colonel or something. We shrugged and muttered "RHIP" (Rank Has Its Privileges), and wondered where they went, the two of them.

We flyers also had a quirky feeling that the enemy might interrupt all these civilized doings. The Japanese were abruptly coming back to life, putting their planes into the sky, day after day. The Aussies had driven them on the ground, and we'd just about taken over the air from them, and I suppose they suddenly faced reality and knew they were going to lose, and decided to make a hell of a fight of it.

One morning on my day off, the heavy ack-ack guns began going off thunderously, their shells climbing high with that echoing whisper that we'd come to consider our true red alert.

I craned my neck and made out, finally, a little shimmer of a dozen or so silver planes in tight formation. Then the bombs whished down over at the airstrip, and the explosions shook us. We hit the slit trenches, and when the explosions stopped we piled into jeeps and headed for the flight line.

Before Pearl Harbor, Americans were told that Japanese fighter pilots couldn't hit anything in the air, and Japanese bombers were way behind ours in accuracy. By now every Beaver could attest that the enemy fighters were not only good planes, but well handled—though obviously the quality of the pilots was falling off. As for the bombers, they had come mostly at night on nuisance raids which were no more—or less—effective than any that our guys pulled off.

But this daylight raid, at high altitude, was a pro job. They'd battered a couple of strips, smashed some parked aircraft, and killed some guys—not in our squadron. They'd also caught us by surprise and gotten clean away, homeward bound, unscratched. The P-40s and P-39s now roaring off the ground were doing so for morale purposes only.

"Bet they'll come tomorrow," said Pete Fletcher, who was now operations officer. "They like to hit on consecutive days. Remember Moresby?" I remembered that the day my plane got clobbered was the second day of scrambling after Japanese raiders.

Next day, Steve and I were both on alert at the flight line, standing by to scramble. And the enemy got through the warning system again. "Wham! Wham! Wham!" went a 90-millimeter antiaircraft gun, giving us a red alert. No yellow—which would have sent us scrambling. Just red, which meant they were here.

"Here they come," someone shouted. "Look up! Straight up!"

I'd looked at bombers many times, but this sight was chilling. Two waves of silver planes, each in a close, neat "vee of vees," sailed smoothly over us at about 25,000 feet. Bright wings and fuselages glinted in the sun—a lovely sight. And they were directly over us. A perfect vertical line dropped from that superb formation would have ended right where we stood.

Every brave Beaver was suddenly in a slit trench, for if a bomber is directly over you, its bombs are well on the way. We could already sense the distant whishing as they fell. Hearing that sound gave me a nasty feeling that the squirm of bodies in the slit trenches were about to take a direct hit. I broke and ran. So did Steve and three others: Eubank, Fisher, and Horochov. Without a word, we five fled away from the trenches, across the dusty kunai, maybe 40 yards from the alert tent.

Then the whishing was so imperative that we simply flung ourselves face down, fingers buried in the grass roots to squeeze ourselves into the very soil. At the last second I twisted myself to look upward, and knew that the planes were *not* directly over the trenches, but over *us*. I knew this as well as knew my name, and I rolled back and murmured my usual last words: "Damn! Damn! Damn!"

Then the bombs started to hit. They fell short of us, and walked straight toward us, the "crumps" turning into crashing explosions, and then coming so close that human ears couldn't accept the sound. I remember a gong going off between my ears. My body jumped. My head was against Fisher's thigh and I felt him jump too, and heard a funny sound from him—a sort of tired sigh.

The air was filled with angry bees, zinging just above our prone bodies, and it stank of chemicals. And then the terrible sounds diminished and stopped, except for the plopping of pebbles and bits of spent shrapnel as they hit the ground. We cautiously raised our heads.

"Is everyone here?" Steve asked in a shaky voice.

We grunted in answer—all except Fisher. I pushed myself up and looked at him.

He was lying very still, on his stomach. He wore no shirt. And in his meaty, muscular back (Fisher was short and hefty) was a deep red crater, crisp and clean, except for an almost square piece of shiny steel in the middle. A wisp of smoke rose from the wound.

I'm glad to say we didn't gabble hysterically about Fisher getting it. We spoke very little. Horachov began to run for the alert tent, then stopped and sat down.

"Something's wrong with my leg," he said. "But we've got to get a jeep to put him on."

Eubank was up in a moment, running through the clearing curtains of dust. And in another moment Barney, the engineering officer, was beside us in a jeep. He had a blanket from one of our cots.

"Where's Eubank?" I asked. Fisher was heavy and had to be handled carefully. We could use many hands, and Horochov was out of it.

"Doctor Mac's got him. Nasty cut on his elbow. Bleeding all over."

Barney and Steve and I bent over Fisher and with a heave got him off the ground and onto the hood of the jeep, where Barney had spread the blanket. Horochov managed to help, but couldn't use one leg. We eased him into the seat next to Barney, and I rolled up his pant leg. A savage gash, low on his calf, was as dry of living blood as a butcher's roast. The bomb fragment that had caught him had cauterized as it cut. I could see tendons and a glint of bone.

The jeep rattled off. I looked at Steve. "You OK?"

He was sitting down, taking off one boot. "I must have stepped in a wet spot running out here," he said. "I've got water in my boot."

He got the boot free and tipped it, pouring from the heel. Bright red. There was a neat slit in the leather and also on the side of his foot.

"Lie down and hold it up," I told him, hoping that would slow the bleeding. Then I went to the tent to get another jeep. I tried to trot, but my legs were very tired. "Steve can't walk," I explained to Herk. "Got a cut on his foot."

Sheehan quickly went to get him. Herkimer looked at me with despair. "Hell, Ted, was it your idea to run out there?"

"'Fraid so," I said. "Pretty dumb."

"'Never leave a slit trench.' Remember that?"

"Oh, stuff it, Herk." He was squadron C.O., but he was also a good friend.

"Are you hurt?" he asked.

"Not scratch one," I answered.

"No damn justice," he said. Then added, "You get the rest of the day off."

"Why? I'm OK."

"Yeah, but look at your plane." He gestured toward the revetments where brownish smoke hung in the still air. It seemed to come from my revetment. I hurried over—my right leg very stiff—and passed a slit trench where a dazed air mechanic was staring down at a bloody bundle of khaki clothes, all that was left of a man.

Nearby, my dear little plane—"Nanette," as I called her—was reduced to a fine, gray ash. Nothing left to mark this residue as an airplane, a veteran, an old-timer who had done her damnedest to fulfill demands that went far beyond her capabilities.

I looked frantically for John, fearing the worst. Then there was his voice, beside me. "You OK, lieutenant?" He'd asked me that question a lot of times, I realized, since I'd known him.

"How about you?" I asked him.

"I was in a slit trench," he said. "Right next to that one." He nodded toward the one with the body.

"Who…" I started to ask.

"Sergeant named McClosky. New guy. Didn't know him very well."

A crew chief, doing his job, taking shelter on the red alert. All SOP, as we called it—standard operating procedure. Only his slit trench was the one, the only one, that a 250-pound bomb had found.

"He took a direct hit," John said, "just like our ship did."

"Poor bastard," I said. "And poor old Nanette."

"She never knew what hit her, lieutenant. Neither of them did."

We watched the last flicker of flames.

"Anyway," John said. "You'll be flying a P-47 soon."

I stared at him. "You kidding me?"

He shook his head. "We're already reading tech sheets about Pratt and Whitney engines. We're going to fly some real airplanes around here."

My right leg was stiff as a board as I walked back to the alert tent. I picked up my gun, and a paperback Shakespeare, and got a ride back to the mess tent to cadge some coffee. Then I stopped by Doctor Mac's medical tent. He was gone, "getting Fisher and a couple of others into hospital," said the sergeant.

"I've got a charley horse or something," I said. "It's all stiffened up. How about an alcohol rub?"

The medic was agreeable. I showed him the area on my right thigh that was stiff. He poured a little alcohol on it, wonderfully cold and soothing.

Then he paused and stared at the place. There was a small smudge of blood on it, and he took some forceps and pulled out a tiny sliver of steel, the size of a fingernail. "Were you in the bombing?" he asked.

I nodded.

"Could I have your name and serial number, please?"

Had I known why he wanted it, I would never have gone along with that. But army life had taught me to shut up and go along with all idiocies because that's what it all is, anyway. I gave him my name and serial number.

And within a few days my parents, innocently going about their lives across the world, in quiet old New England, received an official telegram from the War Department regretting to inform them that their son had been wounded in action. It took me quite a while to answer their anxious and loving letters and assure them that so far, I was just fine.

As if that idiocy wasn't enough, a month or so later I received official notification that I had been awarded the Purple Heart. Well, I'd been "wounded in action," hadn't I? So I got the gong, right along with Fisher and Horochov and Eubank and Steve.

Fisher was too tough to die, but lost full mobility in one side and was discharged. Horochov was out of action for a month until he got enough strength back into his leg to put pressure on the rudder pedal. Steve was fine, and Eubank was quickly patched up.

I tried furiously to keep picking the scab of my "wound," in hopes that I'd be scarred and would have something to show my grandchildren. It didn't do any good. I've never told them I was officially wounded.

"Think of it as getting the Purple Heart for a close call," Steve suggested. That was after we'd gone back that afternoon to the spot in the grass where we'd flattened ourselves. We found the place, imprinted with our bodies. The craters near it were shallow—each a saucer scooped out of grass and soil by a flat burst of shrapnel. The enemy had been using daisy cutters, which go off as soon as they hit a blade of grass. Our bodies had been just under the angle of the outward blast. We paced off the distance from where we had lain to the edge of the nearest crater. We paced long, to make yards. Four paces. Twelve feet.

In a couple of days, Herkimer sent me down to Moresby to pick up a new plane, another Airacobra, and fly it back to Nadzab. It was a Q-model, tight and sweet, and it was mine. But it wasn't a P-47, and John just shrugged and said, "Wait and see."

We went back to strafing and patrolling and scrambling. We strafed Madang, coming in very low and fast because Slit Trench Sam had warned us that Madang had heavy antiaircraft lying in wait. We swept once right over the cluster of thatched roofs and wooden piers, hammering away with all 16 cannon and everything else. My new plane carried a single .50-caliber machine gun in each wing instead of the two .30s that older models had. I felt very formidable.

Years later, I revisited Madang and found a gleaming little tropical town, white buildings, pith-helmeted police directing traffic, a splendid seaside hotel. I bought a postcard and wrote to Steve. "Remember strafing Madang?" I wrote. "Obviously we missed it."

I was shown around the town, and at my request was driven to the site of the Japanese defenses. Here lay the old airfield, guarded at both ends by big antiaircraft guns, still in place, "Used during the Second World War," said the guide.

"My squadron strafed right here," I said to the guide. "We must have flown right over these guns."

"You couldn't have," he said, tersely. "The Japanese would have shot you down."

"I think we did, though," I murmured.

We tangled occasionally with enemy fighters, and often saw them in the distance—smooth, slender shapes against the clouds. They always seemed to gleam like new cars, and the word went around that the Japanese waxed them to make them faster.

Usually, they turned away from us, reinforcing our feeling that they were intent on saving planes. They may also have realized that if they left our P-39s alone, we might very likely crash and burn anyway. I think every squadron in New Guinea lost more planes to accidents than to combat with the enemy.

Generally there wasn't enough left of the pilot to bury, but sometimes we'd follow one of our boys up onto the sloping hillside north of the Markham and stand at attention in uniforms with ties and caps while a service was read over him.

Joe Ryan had always been a good Catholic, and when he bought it on takeoff one morning—his engine quit—Doctor Mac and his medics gathered up enough of him for a burial service. The group padre, who liked to play poker at our squadron, said Ryan deserved a full mass—the works—and so we pilots pulled on the long pants and starched shirts from our footlockers and jeeped up to the hillside.

It was a hot afternoon, even for the island, and on that treeless greensward, the sweat poured down us in small rivers as we stood at attention for what seemed like an hour. The padre went on with his rites, the sun beat down, we stared straight ahead at the stretcher with Ryan lumped under a dark-green tarpaulin—we'd run out of coffins.

We were all aware of Joe's feet sticking out toward us. He had on his GI boots, and one foot was upright the way it should have been, but the other was flat on its side, in a way that would have been impossible if he'd been alive. We stared at those boots, especially the twisted one. We thought about what Ryan's leg must look like, above that distorted foot. And in quick succession six tough, veteran fighter pilots clumped down on the hot grass, blissfully unconscious.

The padre wasn't a cruel man, and anyway, he didn't want to lose his poker buddies, so he hurried Ryan into the ground. Thankfully, we headed back across the valley in our crowded jeeps, tearing off our neckties and opening our shirts to catch the breeze.

And right at the end of another fighter strip, a P-40 roared into the air and turned directly toward us, and suddenly we heard the shocking sound of silence. Its engine had quit, exactly like Ryan's.

Instantly the pilot jettisoned his belly tank. We saw this big, bomb-shaped 110-gallon tank sail right at us. It struck the ground 100 feet from our road and drenched us with high-octane fuel.

We were all cigarette smokers, back in those days, but for once, not one of the eight or so men clinging to that jeep had yet lit a cigarette. Otherwise we'd have quickly joined Joe Ryan.

Dripping, and sick with the stench, we paused to watch the Kittyhawk slide into an emergency landing on another strip. A nice piece of flying and a great deal of good luck. Then we roared away to our campsite. Steve and I quickly stripped off our clothes, reeking with fuel, and with only shorts on drove to the flight line to take a shower. The eight duty pilots who had missed the fun up on the hill complained about our using their water. We told them to shut up and to douse their cigarettes until everyone who'd been sprayed by that fuel tank had come in to wash the stuff off.

We dried off and slipped back into our shorts. "That's the last damn burial service I'm going to," I said, "except maybe my own."

"I wonder how they'd handle it back home," Steve said. "We regret to inform you that your son blew up while attending a funeral."

Chuckling, we drove back to our tent to open a new bottle of issue whiskey.

We all felt like a drink that evening, and our cocktail hour sips evolved into a real "balloon." Everyone but the people in tomorrow's flights—and even some of them—got smashed and we roared out our songs in what we considered superb harmony. It was our own funeral of sorts for Ryan, who had been a most likable guy.

CHAPTER
FOURTEEN

ME AND MY JUG

At the end of 1943, I was sent down to Moresby with five other pilots and there introduced to a hulking new aircraft, so big that its single cockpit looked ridiculously lonely. The Republic P-47 (Thunderbolt) had a 2000-horsepower radial engine with a turbo supercharger. It had broad landing gear that straddled half the width of the strip. It had a roomy cockpit—huge to a P-39 pilot—with a seat that rose and lowered at the touch of a switch. It had eight .50-caliber machine guns, four clustered in each wing, and although it weighed seven and a quarter tons, it could go fast, and far, and high. It was held in the air, the saying went, by Pratt and Whitney and God.

The six of us mortals had seen P-47s many times, but never before up close. Our assignment in Moresby was to learn to fly them, then ferry six of them to Nadzab and teach the rest of the squadron. This would have been a job for Heming, but he'd recently been sent home, kicking and screaming that he didn't want to go. So Steve and Dink and Schriver were chosen for this task, an honor of sorts, and I was included with a couple of others. I was, of course, surprised and pleased. I had never quite outlived my niggling suspicion that as a fighter pilot I was badly overmatched, that the enemy had little to fear from me, that I had survived this long only because I was unbelievably lucky. Here was a gesture of esteem from the authorities in Group Headquarters. They apparently disagreed with my self-appraisal. But then, what did *they* know?

A P-47 pilot from one of the new groups that had arrived on the island met us. He seemed very young, and like all the new crop of GI pilots he was so nice we found ourselves watching our language. He had flown nothing but P-47s, and found it hard to believe that we came from a squadron that flew P-39s. He barely knew what they were. "Engine mounted behind you, isn't it?" he asked. "Doesn't that affect the center of gravity?"

"Sometimes," we answered, tersely. We wanted him to stop treating us like museum specimens and get us into that lofty cockpit.

We spent a couple of hours studying tech orders and learning where switches and "organ stops" were on the dashboard. The cockpit was so roomy we could actually move about in it instead of being trussed in a stooped position. "Hell," said Shriver. "We got ourselves Cadillacs to fly in."

We puzzled over the landing gear. No simple toggle switch here, but a hydraulic system activated by a lever. To safeguard against accidental raising of the wheels, the lever was automatically trapped by a little hook. When you raised the wheels, you flicked open that hook with a finger of your left hand, then you could move the lever. The apparatus was set low beside your seat, so you couldn't readily see it. We learned to feel for it, but of course couldn't work it until our first takeoff.

That came soon. Within an hour and a half, Dink was ready to go. We watched him climb the little steps that snapped back, flush with the fuselage, when his weight went off them. Then there was a whine, a squeal, a prodigious bark of power, and a blast of blue smoke from the engine, and in a moment he was thundering down the strip.

We had thought that all our hours on the Airacobra's tricycle landing gear might have spoiled us for the slightly trickier handling of the old conventional gear, the dragging tail, of the Thunderbolt. But Dink had his tail up in a moment and quickly eased off the strip. He climbed, turned steeply right and left, climbed again to the distant layer of cloud. We heard his engine's full-power roar diminish to a cruising mutter, then die off. He must be stalling the plane. Yes, we saw it dropping and spinning, then coming out neatly, picking up speed and snarling back up in a perfect loop followed by an Immelmann.

More speed and then a slow roll. Then another, a roll and a half, and down he came in a split-S. He turned toward the strip, barrel-rolled over it, then spiraled steeply to the deck and buzzed us, whamming over our heads so low that we smelled his exhaust. Up he went and around, pulling contrails from his wings, then his gear and flaps came down and, his engine murmuring, he slid onto the strip.

Dink, I realized, was our new Heming.

Though his was an impossible act for the rest of us to follow, we were now forced to try. One by one we took off, did our mediocre best, and landed in time for the next guy to take his shot. My turn came all too soon, yet oddly, I was quite confident that I could handle this beast. Dink was a lot better than I was, but not all *that* much.

I climbed up the aluminum mountain to the cockpit, ran a check, heeled the energizer, toed the engager, and the mighty engine, warmed by previous flights, grumbled to life. I released the brakes and it started to trundle. Kicking the rudder pedals steered it in the zigzags that allowed me to see ahead of that monstrous round nose. I could turn sharper by braking one wheel. At the end of the strip I checked the mags, the engine merely purring at the required rpms. Then I rolled straight, locked the tail wheel, lowered the flaps a few degrees as I'd been told, and poured on the coal.

With 2000 horses in the nose, I'd expected heavy torque, but the plane held straight without effort and the tail came up soon, mostly lifted by the prop wash, which, like everything else about a P-47, was gigantic. With the tail up, I could see forward at last. The strip stretched straight before me, rolling under me fast. Then, without help from me, the plane was off. I fumbled for the landing gear lever, clicked away the safety hook, and moved the handle to the Up position. The rush of air took on a slightly different note. Then I felt a small thump, and vibration ceased. I milked the flaps up, closed the little cowl flaps that keep the engine cool on the ground, and as the plane's surface smoothed out, so did the hum of the air.

In a new plane, you listen for the notes and tones that mean climb, cruise, dive, stall, and the phases of landing and taking off, and try to learn this song of the air as soon as you can. It saves a lot of staring at the air speed indicator. You also learn where your nose belongs on the horizon in level, cruising flight. Dink had done all that instinctively and instantly. I did it consciously and carefully. That was the difference between us.

I swung sharp left and right, and realized that this mighty Thunderbolt was a docile, faithful handmaiden, not that gorgeous, murderous call girl named Airacobra. This great aircraft was honest and upright and true, not riddled with disease and given to tantrums and hysterics. I put the big round nose up into a steep climb, and held it for a power stall. The plane hung on its propeller for what seemed an age, then the nose sagged protestingly and the spin reluctantly started. Not being Dink, I kicked out of it quickly, telling myself I'd risk a spin tomorrow.

I soon understood that whereas a P-39 loved nothing better than to return to earth "any old which away," this mighty bird desperately wanted to fly. It hated to stall out and sternly resisted it. Climbing high, it roared with vigor. It flung itself into a loop exuberantly. It rolled inverted effortlessly, then pitched downward in a split-S, howling with joy. But chop the throttle, and it would sag toward the ground, grumbling disgustedly now that the fun was over.

Landing was always the tricky bit for me. I'd finally gained so much feel for a P-39 that I could squeak its tricycle gear on again and again, nose high, one wheel first. But this was a conventional "tail-dragger," designed to be put down on three points. My respect for a decent landing in such an aircraft verged on awe, thanks to experiences as a cadet.

Twice, in primary flight school, I'd ground-looped the Stearman biplane that I trained on, swinging off course after landing, so that the plane pivoted irresistibly on one wheel, dragging—and damaging slightly—one wing. I was retained as an aviation cadet only because the United States badly needed another body, just then. In advanced school, I'd done the same thing in an AT-6. That ground loop had been a night landing, and I'd felt the swing and immediately braked one wheel to straighten out. The brake didn't hold the plane. Around it spun, down went one wing, also one wheel—damage enough for an official investigation.

The accident board judged that I'd reacted correctly to the plane's swing and spared me from "washing out" of cadet training. But landing a tail-dragger remained my secret nemesis, quiescent after all these months of combat missions with a tricycle gear, but ready to spring at me in a split second.

Thinking of the horror of ground-looping this huge plane, this Amazon of fighters, I brought her in gently, holding her straight, lifting her nose, and clumping her down a little hard, maybe, but safe and sound. "Hey, you looked pretty hot up there," said Dink as I clambered down. And I felt vastly pleased.

We flew for two days. My old log book says I got 3 hours of "transition" at Moresby. New planes must have come in during the second day, for on the third—New Year's Day of 1944—we ferried the first '47s back to Nadzab, buzzing the strip with a horrendous racket before landing in front of the entire squadron. It was the perfect moment for me to ground-loop, but I didn't, and my confidence in the Thunderbolt boomed.

Thunderbolt was her official name. Soon pilots called her Thundermug, referring to the chamber pot that, in the 1940s, still lurked under millions of rural American beds. That became Thunderjug, and finally just Jug. That name stuck, mostly because the beefy fuselage had the same profile as the milk jugs we'd known all our young lives.

We quickly started teaching the rest of the Beavers all that we knew about this monster plane. But at the same time there were missions to fly, and we returned to our Airacobras to escort B-25s on a full week of raids along the north coast— but not over Uligan Harbour. A few days later we escorted them again, this time in P-47s.

The Jugs were wonderful. On that escort, two flights hung close over the bombers while the other two, including mine, weaved 8000 or 9000 feet higher. We had a strange new knowledge that we could soar right on to more than 30,000 feet if we wished. We saw some Japanese fighters, but they recognized that milk-bottle shape and didn't want to get close.

Just by being there we were doing our job. A great way to fight a war.

Our planes were painted—the squadron's yellow circling the engine cowling, the numbers stenciled on noses and tails. Again 74 became my own. John and I went over her carefully. John said the engine was easier to get at than the P-39's Allison.

Word came that our whole fighter group would be given Jugs. Even the 39th Squadron, veterans with their marvelous Lightnings, would have to trade them in for Jugs. That outraged the P-38 boys, including Guppy.

He came to see Steve and me, fuming about the idiocies of Fifth Fighter Command and swearing that he'd never give up his superb twin-engine plane to learn to fly "seven and a half tons of shit." As he polished off our carefully hoarded last bottle of whiskey, he promised us portentously that he was getting out of this terrible place instantly, that he had a scheme cooked up, that he was already working on it, that no brass-bound son of a bitch was going to get him into a Thunderbolt.

"What are you going to do?" we asked.

"Drink myself back home," he said.

Steve and I looked at each other, both thinking: By God, it might work.

We moved to a new base, Gusap, in the Ramu Valley, northwest of the Markham Valley. It was open, sitting out there in the kunai with no attempt at concealment, just as though we owned the place. The fact was, we were really on the way to doing just that, even though the ground fighting continued to be a stubborn, messy business, the Japanese clinging bitterly to every scrap of high land. Every day and many nights, we clearly heard the thumping of the Australian 25-pounders up in the hills, battering the enemy, then inching forward and battering some more. In a way, I was sorry not to be helping those guys as we had for so long, strafing and bombing with P-39s. But for us the war had changed.

Our missions were much longer, now that we had the range of the Jugs. We ventured far up the north coast of the island, flying serenely high above the Japanese strips that we had shunned for so long. They were just long, straight smears in the green of the distant jungle, and sometimes we'd see coral dust rise from them as the Tonys took off to investigate us.

They generally were satisfied to look us over from afar. Perhaps they'd been subject to fighter sweeps so often, with their interceptors getting caught on the ground by our subsequent wave of bombers, that they'd become shy of scrambling. But I think this generation of enemy pilots, pale copies of the earlier warriors, simply didn't feel competent to take on the Jugs.

I was just as glad, and I guess most of our old pilots were. My thoughts were more and more on getting home alive. The eagerness of the new men to clobber a bunch of enemy planes and become aces had never affected me very strongly, and now seemed more foreign than ever. I knew that, given the right opportunity—a chance to attack unseen, without a bullet being fired at me in retaliation—I could probably bag an enemy plane. But the missions were cut and dried. Fly up to a target area, stooge around, fly home again. No enemy plane was going to wander into my gunsight and sit there patiently. So best I forget making any score at all. Just get back safely every time, I told myself, and before you know it, you'll be home in lovely, cool, friendly, happy New Hampshire, home to tell my adventures to admiring girls, home in the family womb.

Yet there were moments when a madness swept over me and derailed me from my purposeful track. One day we pulled a sweep right over Wewak—gun-bristling, Zero-buzzing Wewak, Japan's north coast bastion, second only to Hollandia as an enemy base. The whole squadron went, Herkimer leading. I led a flight right next to him. Two other flights hung a little behind us and a fair bit higher. If enemy planes went for the tempting lower flights—Herk's and mine—the others could come down on them, snapping a trap.

We flew high over the whole Wewak area, looking down on a number of Japanese strips, all along that stretch of coast. We got no ack-ack, which indicated that their own planes would be flying. Sure enough, we saw the dust of takeoff as we sailed on northward.

And, sure enough, when we turned around and sailed back again, there were the enemy planes, already 1000 feet above us. We didn't think Tonys could climb that fast, and figured these must be Zekes or Oscars. But they were hard to identify, up against the sun.

They wove around in pairs, the way they liked to do, and we plodded along in fours under them. We watched them and they watched us. They may have been chattering away, but no one spoke on our frequency, so our aerial parade was, to us at least, silent.

I don't know what in the world got into me, but I suddenly swung my flight away from Herk's, nosed down to gain speed, then soared upward, nose high, gunsight searching for a meatball. And when the Japanese fighters flashed into my vision, I crammed down the trigger and felt the thunder of those eight big guns. I think my flight fired with me, but I can't be sure. Things happened too fast.

In a prolonged flash of brightness, every Japanese plane flipped on its back. Here was the illusion of a school of fish suddenly changing diection that I'd seen many times before. Then down they came, split-essing on us, with the same old flames rippling from their silhouetted wings. The nearest of them, their leader, dove straight for me.

I may have fired again, while he was in my sights. But my plane was slopping around, ready to stall, so I banged the stick forward. Down went the nose, and up rushed the blood to my eyes, blurring my vision with a red fog—"redding out," as we called it. I craned around to look at my rudder. The enemy was still on me, but at pretty long range.

My neck twisted around like an owl's. I watched him gain, saw his tracers flick past, and shoved the stick farther forward to increase my dive. I didn't feel excited or scared, just rather interested. I had a superb view of a fleeting aerial moment: one plane diving on another, guns flashing.

Watching the enemy, I kept pushing my nose down and my throttle forward. The giant engine suddenly surged, and I heard a sharp explosion. At about the same time, the enemy plane fell behind, then flicked away. I was going too fast for him to follow without tearing his wings off, Also, our two rear flights were doing their stuff, blazing down on him and his buddies, and I was left to pull out of my dive.

I twisted back to stare at the jungle coming up at me at an incredibly fast rate. A glimpse of my air speed showed 480 miles per hour. But already I was hauling out, easing throttle, wondering where my plane had been hit, hoping a vital piece of it wouldn't fall off, hoping I wouldn't get into what pilots back then called "compressibility," a freezing of the controls when new fighters—usually P-47s—approached the speed of sound in a dive.

That phenomenon, incidentally, explains the old concept of a "sound barrier." It wasn't a barrier at all. Bullets had been outpacing sound for years. But until knife-winged jets cut through the compressed sound waves, they presented a problem, and I was almost able to report on it, firsthand.

True to type, however, my powerful survival instincts kicked in, enabling me to haul out before testing this mysterious barrier—and splashing myself into the Sepik River rain forest. My Thunderbolt wrenched itself upward while all the blood that had had been flung into my head was abruptly sucked downward toward my feet. I clenched my stomach muscles to keep enough up there to let me see. And through the misty beginnings of blackout, I made out the unmistakable milk-jug shapes of my squadron, above and slightly ahead.

I was unscathed. The only trouble was that explosion. Having been hit, and also near-missed, I was sensitive to such sounds, yet also wary of passing judgment on them.

Herkimer's voice came in: "Park, check in, will you? Park? You OK?"

"I'm fine," I answered. No need for all the Roger-Wilco-Over-and-Out crap. The Japanese knew where we were, and we knew where they were. "I'm under you, Herk, heading up."

I saw the lead plane weave and bank as he peered down at me. "I got you, Park," he said.

I added throttle and climbed to catch up. The plane lumbered into position, and I saw the rest of my flight sorting themselves out and coming together with me. Our little soiree had apparently busted our formation all to hell-and-gone. But I saw no gaps in any of the four flights. I wondered if we'd hit any of the enemy planes.

Once formed up, we began to climb for more altitude. And at about 15,000 feet, my engine stuttered and I fell away. I called Herk: "This is Park. I can't hold power. Engine may have been hit."

"I'll stay with you," he said. "White Flight, take the lead. I'll fly Park's wing."

Throttling back helped restore some wallop to my engine. But as we continued, it roughened again, badly. I had to throttle back some more and had trouble holding altitude. Herk flew all around me, looking me over. "You're throwing oil pretty badly from the bottom of your cowling," he said. "You may have taken a bullet there. Can you keep flying?"

"So far so good," I said.

We rumbled along over the endless swamp that seems to fill all of New Guinea as you fly southeast from Wewak toward the Ramu Valley. The roughness returned and I eased the throttle back until it smoothed out. Of course I lost a little more altitude. Herk stayed with me. We were now down to about 8000 feet.

"Do you want to leave it?" he asked. It was an obvious question, and he tried to conceal its implications by making it sound conversational. Of course I'd been mulling it over. But the swamp down below was perhaps the world's worst place to bail out. And right then the engine was running fine.

"Not yet," I said.

He was close on my left wing and I saw him simply nod his head at me.

We got past the worst of the swamps, and now the land rose to meet us. The next time the engine began missing, I had to come down to within about 4000 feet of a tangle of knotty little hills. Still terrible country to bail out into, but at least not a swamp.

"I'll be right with you, if you decide to go out," Herk said. "Just tell me so I can get some bearings."

I nodded.

Hell! Hitting the silk! Second biggest moment in flying, after buying the farm. I'd always put it more or less out of mind—a nasty possibility, obviously not worth worrying about. It wasn't the jumping out of a moving plane that concerned me; I'd learned to picture that. It was the long walk home.

Even from where we now flew, well clear of the swampland, the odds of reaching any outpost were stacked against me. They'd have improved if I'd been younger, newer, fresher, fatter, stronger, braver, brighter; but I was a scrawny, underweight veteran, dependent on pills to keep malaria at bay, unaccustomed to walking anywhere if I could ride, so fatalistic I was beginning to believe in predestination. I was a lousy bet in the survival stakes.

The engine rattled and gasped again, and I throttled back and sagged down to 3500 feet. I'd have to leave at about 1000 in order to control my 'chute at all after it opened. Let's see: You're supposed to pull the shrouds down in the direction you want to go, aren't you? Or is it the other way?

And what direction were we thinking about? Right here, the ground was laced with tiny streams, a tangle of brooklets meeting and swelling—the capillaries of the jungle's circulation system. God, not *here!* Please give me a little grass, a patch of kunai. OK?

"Better country ahead," said Herk in my earphones. "Stick with it a little longer."

Sure enough, the land flattened over the plane's nose, and I caught the gleam of a river—the Ramu at last. We labored toward it. This was better country, and when we finally reached it, I was still showing 3000 feet on my altimeter. The needle was set for Gusap, and this wasn't much higher. I settled myself more comfortably, realizing how stiff and cramped I'd become with endless tension. My flying suit was sweat-soaked. But then, it usually was during a mission.

Now I began to feel that I might get home if I hit the silk. Give me a river and I could make a raft. Boats I understood. But the Japanese presented problems this far up the Ramu. They would surely have patrols here, probably even communication routes. If they spotted my 'chute, they'd naturally wander over to see what was going on, and if they found me, they'd kill me perfunctorily—"No hard feelings, Yankee dog." Blam!

Of course I could fight back. I had my Colt automatic, and I could fire it if I remembered to cock it first and release the safety, and if the thing wasn't so rusty that it either went off with a dull click or blew up in my hand. Or I could throw it at the enemy. It was nice and heavy.

The ground slid by under our wings. At the slightest increase in throttle the engine gave every sign of simply stopping dead. Constantly reducing power kept it running, but rougher and rougher. I sank farther down: 2500 feet; 2000 feet. The rate of descent seemed much quicker. My decision was coming up too fast. Jump or crash-land?

Hey! How about crash-landing? Let's see: Wheels would stay up, flaps would be all the way down and the nose held high as we settled....Where would we settle? No flat spot down there; no line of beach along the twisting river; no level meadow.

A memory came back of a day at Charters Towers when Steve and Guppy and I—getting over dysentary—took a jeep to explore around the base. As we passed the end of the strip, a B-25 thundered off and headed over us, and we stopped to watch it pass, maybe 100 feet above. And as we watched, one engine quit cold. We could see the pilot and copilot, working frantically, trying to restart, trying to feather, trying to keep flying on one engine with a full load.

And then the plane sagged toward the trees and we heard and felt the ground-shaking "crump," far off in the forest where no road went. We couldn't get in to help. No one could. So we tore back to the base to tell the people in the tower where to search. They knew, anyway, for the smoke still rose in a twisted column, a mile away. I'll always remember those two strained faces—so intent on surviving, so busy, so absorbed in a useless effort.

That would be my face as I crash-landed, my plane nose-high with stilled propeller, its fragile belly reaching for bouldered, tree-stumped, gullied ground at 85 miles an hour. Damn! Damn! Damn!

Eighteen hundred feet. For a blessed moment the engine ran quite well. I found myself holding my breath as though the act of breathing would bring on the now terrible roughness. Sixteen hundred feet. My climb indicator showed 100 feet a minute descent. Six minutes before bailout. Sixteen minutes before crash-landing. I'm sure I didn't really figure that out sitting in that cockpit, pouring with sweat. I just felt it, the way a pilot does.

"If you keep this up, you'll make the strip," said Herk. "Want to try?"

"Yes," I said.

Suddenly I knew that was the right answer.

Herk's voice got very busy calling Gusap control, asking them to clear the strip, that a crippled Beaver was coming straight in from the northwest.

I felt fine. The decision had been made, and I was committed, and the hell with it all. Of course I'd get in all right.

The plane seemed as relieved as I was. We hummed on at low rpms, sinking slowly, but now with assurance that it would be OK. As I passed 1000 feet, the end of the Gusap strip was in sight. Herk stayed close. "Wheels down at the last minute," he said. "You'll be fine. I'm right here to watch."

At 500 feet I was just about right for my final approach. But I was too fast. I eased down flaps.

"Wheels now," said Herk. "You're coming in hot."

The wheels thumped down. And as though their drag was the last straw for it, the engine quit cold, the prop slowing its whirl, barely turning in the slipstream. "I'm dead-stick," I said on the radio.

"I know," said Herk. "Just land it and let it run off the end of the strip. You're home."

I did what he said. It was a very hot landing, and it was embarrassing to run off the end of the strip and sit there in the grass until the operations jeep came out to get me. People told me afterward that dead-stick landings are often too hot. Pilots overcompensate.

The plane was fine except for a hole in the cowling. A piece of a cylinder head had blown right through it when the engine surged. I was shamefaced when I met Barney after he'd looked it over with his engineering crew. But he said it wasn't my fault. "Those engines are built to take anything you guys give them," he said. "If they don't, it's their fault, not yours."

It's an indication of the Jug's legendary toughness that mine got me home that day, even though a useless piston was slatting around in a ruptured cylinder, deep in its innards. Later I was to see a Jug get a little too low while buzzing the sea off Moresby, and strike the surface of the water. Smothered in a white cloud of spray, it slowed down fast, then broke free and climbed away, streaming and steaming.

The pilot got back to his strip, landed, and taxied in. I learned that he was deeply embarrassed at the noise he made. His engine was bellowing at high rpms to keep him rolling, for his propeller didn't have much thrust. About 16 inches of each of its four blades were bent back 90 degrees.

But his faithful Jug—like mine—brought him home. It was the St. Bernard of all fighters.

The P-47 was weak in only one way. It too often blew a tire on takeoff or landing. I suppose that wartime rubber was synthetic, or old; anyway, it couldn't take the heat of high speed on tropical strips of coral or steel matting with more than seven tons pressing on it.

Usually it was only the tail wheel that blew, and often we never felt it go. But sometimes it was a main wheel, and the plane would slew off course, like a car with a blowout. If the prop struck an embankment and stopped dead, all that fuel pouring into the hot engine could flare up, and that flash of fire could set the whole plane off into a ball of flame.

One new man who blew a main wheel on takeoff got caught by the initial flash fire. He had his goggles up on his helmet and his oxygen mask flapping below his chin, and the flash toasted his face before he could snap open his harness and get out. He did manage to scramble clear of the plane before it exploded, and he was unhurt except for a very bad sunburn. From then on we took off with goggles down, masks up, and gloves on. Also, we now took off one by one with about 1000 feet between us, instead of by element, two planes side by side, as we used to in the 'Cobras.

My right wheel blew one morning as I was taking off at the head of Red Flight. I chopped the throttle and fumbled for the fuel shutoff valve as my plane veered inexorably toward the ditch on the right side of the runway. I couldn't hold it, and we slumped into it with a thud. And then I was out of there, running for my life, waiting to feel the heat of the explosion.

No flash fire. No explosion. Once again my marvelous instinct for cowardice had saved my skin.

But two other old pilots had a close call on a coral strip. Foxey Schriver and Dick Burnham—the man who met the pygmies—were going off together on some special flight, and Foxey, leading, blew a main wheel and ground-looped on the loose coral. He ended up skewed across the strip with a broken wheel, while a white fog of coral dust hid him.

Burnham, thundering straight at him on his takeoff, realized that it was too late to chop his gun and slow down. Instead, he hauled back on his stick, and his Jug staggered into the air, skimmed right over Schriver, then mushed down on the other side and continued its takeoff run. Foxey said he could almost touch one of Burnham's spinning wheels as it brushed over his head.

We thought up ways to lessen the blowouts, like cutting little vanes in the wheel rims so they'd begin spinning as soon as they were lowered for a landing, thus lessening the abrupt friction of motionless rubber hitting the ground at 90 miles an hour. We also began toeing the brakes as we retracted the landing gear on takeoff, so the tires wouldn't wear by spinning against obstructions in the wheel wells.

Nothing worked particularly well, but eventually the number of blowouts eased off. Probably changes were made at the various plants that built these Republic planes back in the States. Our confidence in them had never been badly shaken. Now it increased to the point where even I undertook a long hop in bad weather without my silver dollar.

Many of us carried good-luck charms, and mine was a silver dollar. I always carried it in a pocket of my shorts when I flew, and so far, so good. Then one day I had to fly down to Moresby for a dental appointment. It was my turn to have a wisdom tooth out.

Steve drove me to the line, where I would take my own plane, calling myself "Beaver Special." The weather was murky and the meteorologists reported clouds over most of the island.

As I jumped out of the jeep, I missed the feeling of a hard object against my right thigh. I paused and reached through the slit in my flying suit to find the pocket of my shorts. No silver dollar.

"If you find my silver dollar in the tent, save it for me," I told Steve.

"You mean you haven't got it?"

"It may be caught up in another pocket."

"Well, take it easy in this weather."

"Sure. Thanks for the ride. See you tomorrow."

Alone in the plane, I wondered about good-luck charms. I was too rational to think they did any good, but I realized that my coin might well bolster my fragile confidence. Still, if it was lost, so be it. Now was the time to learn to get along without it.

I climbed out of Gusap and found a hole that took me into clear sunlight. Then I laid a course for the coast a little west of Moresby. There were always some clouds over the island; there were often some over the sea. But along the coast the clouds were always patchy. You could generally find a hole and go down to the deck if you had to. You could always find a little visibility down there, enough to get you onto a strip without resorting to instruments—which in our fighters weren't maintained and weren't much help. Also, fighter pilots were pretty lousy on instruments.

It worked out about as I'd thought. I found the cloud cover patchy over the coast, let down and slid along looking for Moresby off my left wing. But the visibility got worse and worse. I could see nothing except the shore directly below me, and I flew that way, looking down, watching for a sign of Moresby, and wondering about my silver dollar.

And then, under my left wing, the shore moved abruptly in to form a little bay, and in the middle of it, clearly visible in the shallow water, was a ditched B-17. I knew that old wreck well from having flown over it almost daily back in our Moresby days. The bomber had apparently run out of fuel on its final approach into 7-mile. It had landed in the bay—Bootless Bay—and its remains pointed like an arrow toward the strip, a lasting monument to pilot error.

Thankfully, I pivoted my fighter over the ditched bomber and followed the path which it pointed out. Immediately, the end of 7-mile loomed before me, and I chopped the gun, dropped flaps and wheels, and slid in nicely, an apparition out of the fog to the few people who saw me.

So much for my lucky dollar. Flying home next day, in bright sunlight, I wondered whether yesterday's flight would have been so tough if the dollar had been in my pocket. Yet the real luck was finding that no-longer Flying Fortress. The dollar didn't do that. Fate did it; random chance did it. God did it, just as God had kept me in the air from Wewak to Gusap that day when one of Pratt and Whitney's 18 cylinders had blown during our little soiree.

For all I knew, God may have arranged for that bomber pilot to run out of fuel and ditch exactly on course for his home strip. Why? Just to save my frightened little ass? Why me? Predestination?

I hadn't had time to think about all this yesterday as I landed out of the gloom. But now, in serene sunlight, with the Japanese many miles away, I nodded my helmeted head up at God from my cockpit, to say "Thanks, sir." Just in case. The nonchalant, semiatheism that had suited me in peacetime sometimes felt uncomfortable in this strange and violent time and place.

CHAPTER
FIFTEEN

RITE OF PASSAGE

By March 1944, we were clearly going to win the war, and the only remaining mystery was: When? I'd known enough early days of feebleness to have sampled the antic madness that accompanies a wave of disaster. I had found the chaos of those times novel, exciting, even rather pleasant. The insanity cleared away life's foggy trivia, like the web of small half-truths that help support your self-esteem. Instead, you faced a sharp-edged, elemental decision: survival or death. In that atmosphere, simple and clear, you did your best, and stopped worrying what people would think, years later. Being a New England Yankee with a built-in burden of suppressed guilt, I found the sense of imminent defeat quite relaxing.

Now we were constantly reminded of victory—inevitable, if not yet imminent. A British commando officer dropped by our squadron to point out that if we bailed out and were taken prisoner we should forget the old rote of revealing only name, rank, and serial number to our captors.

"Tell them anything," said the Brit. "You don't know enough yourselves to do us any harm, and we're going to win, no matter what you tell them, so sing like a bird if it'll save your necks."

He said we should wear no insignia when we flew (few of us did), and if captured we should always give our rank as lieutenant. No higher. "They know that lieutenants are just small fry," he said, "and they'll be more apt to let one off the hook than a major or a colonel."

He added that Japanese interrogators loved stories that contained elements of pornography. "Tell them about your sexual exploits in Sydney," he suggested. "They like to hear all the details, so fill your stories with fantasies and crude language. Then they may leave you alive as a source of entertainment."

The commando was one of those cultured warriors who spoke matter-of-factly about incredible danger and bloodshed but always in a coolly modulated, afternoon-tea-with-the-vicar voice. "Avoid capture if you can," he told us. "The enemy is short of food, and kills his prisoners in order not to feed them. So if you're down in his area, lie low during the day and then get away at night. If you come up on a Jap soldier then, use your knife, not your gun. No shooting."

We looked at him in surprise. It hadn't occurred to any of us that our knives, so proudly honed to shave our forearms for all these months, might have to be used against a person. Parachute straps, yes. But human beings?

He read the question in our faces. "You do know how to use a knife, don't you?"

We were silent, ashamed of our ignorance.

"Look here." He moved over to Mendoza, who was standing uneasily near him. "You come up behind your victim—do you mind, old chap?—get a hand under his chin, pull his head back, like this, and slip your blade into the soft spot just above the collar bone. Right here." Mendoza squirmed as a finger probed the little pocket of soft flesh between his clavicle and scapula. "If you've got it right, the knife should go in easily, almost by its own weight. Once it's fully in, turn the blade until you feel blood on your hand. You'll know the feeling. Wet and hot...."

And as the Oxford-Cambridge accent continued, I noticed a universal greenish shade come over every face in the squadron. Three tough-talking Americans, each quite ready to blast a dozen Nipponese planes from the sky, rose abruptly and left the assembly tent. *Knifing?* The hell with that!

The British commando left us more determined than ever not to be taken prisoner. But our release from the old stricture of telling our captors nothing was most welcome. John Wayne wouldn't have approved, but we did.

Another indication of our winning the war was an airshow, put on by our great ace, Richard Bong, right there at Gusap.

The purpose was originally to bolster the confidence of new pilots in the aircraft they were assigned for missions. Douglas Bader, the great British ace who flew superbly with two artificial legs, used to put on an exhibit for American aviation cadets to give them confidence in their planes. Out here it was Dick Bong, demonstrating that his P-38, which had the reputation of handling like a Mack truck, could do wonderful things even on one engine if you understood her and loved her.

Dick Bong was an affable young midwesterner who came out to New Guinea with the unusual asset of P-38 "time"— actual experience in flying the Lightning. He was assigned to the 49th Fighter Group, flying P-40s, but started flying with our 35th Group because our 39th Squadron was the first in New Guinea to get P-38s. He started scoring victories with us, and kept going after he reverted to his own outfit.

Bong had three tours of duty in New Guinea, scored and scored, and by 1944, was a famous young man with war correspondents trekking around to have a look at him. The Fifth Air Force set him up in a special flight of aces in four red-nosed '38s. They scored and scored. Sometimes on days off, Bong put on his own private airshow for new pilots and for VIPs.

So here he was at Gusap with a visiting movie starlet crammed into a makeshift seat behind him, because she wanted so very badly to be able to tell her friends in Hollywood that she'd flown with the great ace. Some of us Beavers watched, not just to see Dick fly, which was old stuff, but to catch a glimpse of the starlet, a radiant little thing with perfume that nailed us half a mile away.

Extremely mindful of his soft, aromatic cargo, Bong edited his usual wild-ass performance down to a most gentlemanly flight—only one loop and a couple of easy barrel rolls. Then he came in for his usual showboat landing, designed to quell the fears of P-38 kids who doubted the capabilities of the big plane if and when an engine quit.

He howled over the strip, down on the deck, then pulled up sharply, killing *both* engines and feathering the props. On momentum alone, he coasted up and gradually over in a lazy, eerily silent loop. While inverted, the plane sprouted wheels and flaps, then whistled on down in a controlled dive toward the end of the strip. With a couple of sideslips and a fishtail, Bong killed off his speed and kissed the matting. His plane rolled along the runway, slowing fast. It had just enough life left to turn toward the assembled brass, gathered outside the alert tent. And as it finished its roll, Bong touched the brakes so the nose bobbed down, making a little bow to us fans.

It was quite a show, even though most of us had seen it before. We gave Dick a big hand as he climbed out. Then he turned to offer help to the beautiful creature from Hollywood.

She wouldn't get out of her seat. Not until, she explained, the crowd had gone. Major Bong had caused her to wet her lacy little panties, and she refused to arise until she could scurry off, unseen. I suppose it cooled her interest in Bong.

We had little time for shows at Gusap, now that the Jugs rendered us true aerial warriors. Yes, even I managed to score, and I basked in the glory of it and relished every hint of kudos I could gather. Many servicemen avoid reliving the details of their moments of action. Not I. I always loved talking about my sole victory, and still, like the Ancient Mariner, clutch at possible listeners and let them have it:

Returning from an escort to Wewak, I was dutifully weaving my flight above the huge B-24s when my wingman called in. He was a recent replacement, and he now had an oil leak and said he could barely see through his smeared canopy.

The mission was all but over, our four flights well on the way out of enemy country. So, "Beaver Leader from Red One," I called. "I'll lead Red Two home. Red Three and Four can join your flight."

Beaver Leader—I think it was Steve that day—agreed. With my wingman firmly in place, I broke away from the weaving flights and headed straight for Gusap. The new pilot anxiously watched me every second.

We soared over the great swampland, and then the terrible little hills. When at last I saw the sweep of the Ramu Valley, I called sector and told them I was coming in early with a snafu, and the two of us would be with them soon.

"Beaver Red Leader," said sector, "keep clear, keep clear. We have bandits in the area."

"Roger," I gulped, wondering if it was a big raid, or what. I leveled out and started a wide turn to kill time.

Sector soon called again. "Beaver Red, you are now clear to land. Two bandits have left us heading northwest. Keep a sharp lookout."

Even as I acknowledged, I saw them: two dark-green Tonys below us scurrying over the hills. Hard to see against the jungle, except for crimson circles, outlined in white, on their wings. They must have been strafing, I decided, and were racing for home.

The pair were in line astern, a long gap between them. We were between them and the sun. A cloud also obstructed their view back and up. I'd only recently decided to wait for a perfect chance to shoot down an enemy plane. If I had really meant it, then here it was.

On the other hand, I had this kid with the oil leak to shepherd home. Moral dilemma. The Christian thing was to take care of the lost sheep, right? But I was the product of exhaustive and expensive training for the purpose of destroying enemy aircraft, and here was the best opening a fighter pilot could ever hope for.

It took me half a second to make my decision. "Orbit right here," I told my wingman. "I'll meet you later."

And I stood on one wingtip and peeled off, thundering out of the sun, whipping down from behind a cloud, falling in astern of the nearest Tony. "I've got you, you bastard," I muttered into my oxygen mask.

From then on, I thought of things and did things in instants, but the thoughts and actions seemed to take as long as I do now to describe them. I got my plane straightened out, its throttle still crammed forward. The dark silhouette of the Tony's wings and fuselage in my gunsight grew larger.

Had I forgotten anything? My belly tank had been jettisoned back over Wewak, when we chased some would-be interceptors away from our bombers. The plane was trimmed; its ball and needle centered, so it wasn't slipping. Gun switches were on. But perhaps I'd better clear my guns after all that time at high altitude.

I pressed the trigger, and all eight went off just fine. Then a funny thing happened. As my tracers reached toward the target, I couldn't stop firing. It occurred to me that when the Japanese saw the tracers, he'd know he was was too low to dive away, so he'd probably haul up, twist around, and shoot back, as I would have tried to do in that situation. I figured I'd better get him now, even though the range was long.

I kept holding the trigger down and the target kept flying straight and level in my sight. And then the dark silhouette flashed with spots of light as my bullets began to hit home. For a moment the Tony turned and skidded in a sideslip, and I could see—almost feel—my converged hail of steel smashing into that fuselage, shoving it sideways. Great pieces of airplane came off it and flicked past me,

And then the plane rolled lazily on its back and dropped like a rock straight into the jungle.

To my surprise, a parachute blossomed abruptly in the smoky air where the enemy plane had been flying. I'd read that the Tony had thicker armor plate than the Jug, and here was proof that a Japanese pilot had survived a pretty good clobbering.

When the stricken plane passed out of my gunsight, it was replaced by the other Tony, too far away, but getting closer fast as I sped after it. Now my tracers looped out for it. Surely it would turn and come at me. It was the leader, the old hand who knew just what to do. The other one, the one I'd managed to get, had to be a new guy, fresh out of flight school.

New guy? Uh-oh. Suddenly I remembered my wingman, and duty now gave me serious pause. I held the trigger a moment longer, just in case I got lucky. I thought I saw hits, but I had to break away and head back toward my rendezvous.

Immediately, I spotted the parachute, under my right wing, dropping away with the pilot clutching the shrouds.

The Japanese shot at our parachutists whenever they could, and our policy was to shoot at them if they were coming down in their own territory and so might fly again. If they were floating down over our territory, they might prove useful as POWs, so we were advised to let them land and get captured.

Well, this area was a mix. Japanese patrols roamed it, and Aussie commandos were there to meet them. I probably should have killed my poor little bugger, but the idea repulsed me. It suddenly seemed imperative to just do the natural thing, and for me that was to slide right past him without firing, and then to lie about it, afterward. I could report that it was impossible to turn tightly enough to get my sights on him.

I must have passed within 50 feet of the Japanese pilot. He was a youngster, atabrine-yellow, like all of us, his black hair cut short except for sideburns. His flying suit looked like mine. He was expressionless, but I could see his eyes follow me as I roared by. What should I do? I wondered. Salute? Give him the finger?

I just looked at him through my goggles, and for a moment we locked eyes.

I searched the sky for my wingman, but had no time to worry about him because someone now appeared to be shooting at *me*. I could hear the snapping of shots, and tracers flashed past my wings. Was there a third enemy plane?

Craning from side to side, I spun my head around like an owl, but found no plane on my tail. The Jug had a little rearview mirror above the cockpit canopy, and I stared at it from every angle and saw nothing but empty sky and once a fleeting glimpse of my own face. I'd pushed my goggles up, and there I was, eyes intense, forehead pale and deeply etched by worry lines.

The mystery shooting stopped. I learned later that when they've been fired steadily, those big machine guns will "cook off," firing a few additional shots by themselves, simply because their barrels are too hot.

Certain that the skies were at last friendly, I called my wingman, and found him sliding into formation. We flew to Gusap and I watched him land and then landed myself. Not until then did I realize I might have pulled off a victory roll, the traditional—and by then highly illegal—way to broadcast a score. No matter. I might well have killed myself doing it, and then I'd have missed all the fun of telling everyone that I'd accomplished the rite of passage, and they could call me Killer Park and give me some damn respect.

So I jabbered away to my good friends before reporting to Intelligence, and they lionized me with hugs and slams on the back, and a hefty shot of whiskey. And then my wingman approached. I barely knew the youngster, but we all had some doubts about his capabilities in a fighter. His oil leak wasn't the first little accident to prevent his finishing a mission. But, hell, I had a lousy record of snafus—that lasting carburetor trouble, and the time the door of my '39 wouldn't close—so who was I to kick about this kid?

"I stayed with you," he said. "I saw your Tony go down. I saw you shoot at the second one, and I shot too, and it went down. Did you see it?"

I looked at him, wide-eyed. "You were *with me?*"

He nodded. "If you confirm my kill, I'll confirm yours."

"Sure," I said. "What the hell?"

I knew I didn't need more confirmation than the film in my gun camera. But if it meant so much to him, I'd tell a standard lie, confirming something unlikely in order to keep morale high and make all the Moms back home in the States feel good about the war.

The truth is, I don't have the faintest idea if what's-his-name shot down the second Tony or not. I never saw him on my wing or behind me. I thought I was alone. His claim now gives me an odd feeling. The way he brought it up was as though he thought *I* was going to claim it. He may have made his claim only because I didn't. For fleeting moments I have since wondered if my last burst at that distant shape did indeed go home. It's faintly possible that I shot down two planes that day, within seconds of each other.

Wow! If I'd claimed them both, I might have been a whiz-bang hero, sporting a Silver Star and burdened by an overwhelming ego. I'd have probably stayed in the air force, flown jets, gone to Korea a few years later, and doubtless gotten myself killed. Ah, fate, fate!

My wingman was transferred out of the squadron soon after that. He ended up flying transports. I never saw him again.

I often wonder about the Japanese pilot. Did he get down all right? Did he survive the war? If so, he owes me.

As it happened, my one glorious victory probably did help change my life. Not long after it, I was made senior flight leader and assistant operations officer, posts which I never realized existed until I was named to them, and which I don't think deserve capital letters. However, being in Squadron Operations, I got a phone call from Group Operations one day in March. Six pilots from the 35th Fighter Group were to make an extended ferry trip to Australia to pick up new Jugs— the beautiful new P-47 D-models with bubble canopies. Hot stuff, right off the drawing boards.

"I want two pilots from each of our squadrons to take on this detached service," said the colonel. "I want one old guy and one new kid. You pick 'em out from the 41st, OK."

"OK," I said, thinking of names.

"Hey, Park," said the colonel. Since I'd scored, he was all buddy-buddy. "When was your last leave?"

"I'm about due," I said.

"Then make yourself the old pilot," he said. "This could be a nice trip. Pick a new boy to go with you."

I picked Tom Mueller, an attractive, competent youngster from Illinois who had arrived in our last shipment of replacements. He flew well and he showed a spark of leadership. Also, he was a good companion, funny and lively and bright. In no time we were packed and away, heading down to Nadzab. There we met the others: two from the 40th Squadron, two from the 39th.

One of them was Guppy. His snarls about the P-47 had done no good, and he hadn't quite succeeded yet in his campaign to guzzle his way home. Now his squadron, the 39th, had grudgingly given up its wonderful P-38s so the whole fighter group could service the one type. Guppy was now a Jug pilot. No matter. He really thought only about getting sent home.

We gathered in a briefing room, the six of us, and a young major came out to brief us about our trip. We looked at him in astonishment: the famous Dick Bong.

"You guys could be in for a great ferry trip," he said. "As you know, usually we get our planes from Brisbane. But this time it looks as though you'll have to go all the way down to Melbourne for them. It's a great place. Not many Americans. Good luck."

Bong would end up the highest-scoring American ace, with 40 planes to his credit. But he was just another fighter pilot, and we talked the same language. We asked him questions, and he told us a bit about himself. "I'm a lousy shot," he said. "I have to get right on the other guy's tail and hang there, and pretty soon I can't help but hit him. I have to fly pretty well to do that."

He was wonderfully modest and frank, and by the time we left for Australia, we felt we had made friends with a very decent, unassuming man. But our mission was first in our thoughts and we were all eager to get on with it.

CHAPTER
SIXTEEN

LAST DAYS OF A
FIGHTER PILOT

Bong was right. We hopped a ride to Garbutt Field in Townsville, picked up six Jugs, and ferried them down to Brisbane. There we got orders to catch an evening plane to Melbourne.

We were overjoyed at avoiding Sydney, for once, and lolled back happily in a nearly empty civilian transport plane, humming peacefully southward through the darkening evening sky. Each of us took a turn up forward in the "greenhouse," chatting with the captain and first officer and putting in a little time at the controls. Then we were on the ground, ready to make a mighty splash in this unknown territory.

Our noisily high-spirited entry into Melbourne had no impact at all on this huge, sprawling, peaceable city. Through the magic of military communications we found ourselves billeted at the Commercial Travelers Club downtown and, impressed with its Victorian demeanor, quickly adapted ourselves to quiet propriety. Our earliest explorations uncovered a series of splendid bars within the club, matched by dozens more outside it. The Victorian beer was memorable, and the food ample and suitably protein-rich.

The girl problem puzzled us. In the heart of town there was a Hotel Australia, just as there was in Sydney, but it didn't have a "snake pit." So where were we supposed to pick up girls? We put our problem to the Fifth Air Force engineers and test pilots who were getting our planes ready to go north, and they showed us the ropes.

You generally didn't pick up girls off a Melbourne street, they said. Usually you just sort of met them the way you would back home. Plenty of people here still asked Americans home for dinner, a hospitality long forgotten in Yank-jaded Sydney. And there was a small American air force officers' club in a wealthy section of the city called Toorak.

The engineering people had another bit of news for us: Our new planes were not ready and might not be for quite a while. They had come over disassembled, on the deck of a freighter, and pieces of them were missing. The few that were flyable had oil leaks. So: "Sorry, you guys. You'll just have to wait here in Melbourne."

Sorry? We were overjoyed.

Gradually, we six went separate ways, though always checking in with one another at our billet. Guppy and I spent one hazily remembered day trying to sample every whiskey that the Commercial Travelers Club stocked. King George IV ranked high, as I recall.

We soon checked out that officers' club in Toorak. It was a spacious old house with lawns and shrubbery, and it held the essentials: bar, juke box with new records, a room for dancing, another for tables, pictures of aircraft on all the walls. Entering the place, you were always greeted by an attractive girl. When that happened on our first visit, Guppy looked at me with wild surmise. "You don't suppose...," he said.

But no. Quite obviously the hostesses had been carefully selected to fit the probity (outward, at least) of Toorak. We danced with them to new songs from the States. We made new friends.

We met fellow flyers and their guests who dropped in at this pleasant old house while on often mysterious assignments in Melbourne. This city, host to General MacArthur in the very early days of the Japanese war, and to the First Marine Division before and during the battle for Guadalcanal, had become an important link in Allied logistics. But it retained its old Victorian character, its social amenities, its dignity, its manners. Melbourne had no carousing, leave-town section like Sydney's Kings Cross. And it may be to our credit that we didn't miss it a bit.

We guessed that the busy, purposeful officers of every Allied nationality who met at the club were probably doing more to win the war than we were, flying our scary little planes in harm's way. But those lovely hostesses liked us better.

Guppy went wild for Nancy, a radiantly beautiful girl, and managed to line up a future date. He, generous soul, wanted to include me. So Nancy persuaded an old friend of hers to try a blind date. The four of us roistered happily at a party that the test pilots threw at their flat.

Another night we ventured into a night club called the Embassy. Melbourne had a wartime stricture barring nighttime drinking, but everyone turned a blind eye on smuggling booze into clubs, and we did so with zeal. Having been brought up in Prohibition days, Guppy and I quickly recalled the word "bootlegger," and put the idea to the test. We found that flying boots served handsomely—a bottle in each.

This was March, early autumn, and the cool southern climate struck savagely at our skinny, thin-blooded bodies. What with hard drinking and little sleep, Guppy was soon besieged by a cold and I came down with laryngitis. One day we agreed on making our evening brief and our sleep long.

"I'll see if Nancy can join us for dinner," sniffled Guppy.

"I don't have a date," I croaked.

"Who cares? It's just for dinner."

Nancy showed up, always a delight. We went to a restaurant for our dose of protein.

"My sister's off-duty tonight," said Nancy. "Maybe she'll join us."

"You have a sister?" I whispered.

"She's a nurse trainee. Almost finished. She's home for the first time in a week."

"Do you think she'd come?" asked Guppy, fighting off a sneeze.

Nancy rose and went to find a telephone.

"I don't want to get into this," I rasped to Guppy. "I need some sack time."

"I need it too. This climate's killing me. But if she can come, we can at least say hello." Guppy always perked up at the prospect of meeting another girl.

Nancy came back, and looked at me. "She says she's too tired to go out. She says she has laryngitis, like you. But she's home. So we'll go there, and you can meet her."

I didn't want to meet her, but I couldn't very well tell that to her sister. We went. We took a cab, and it cost a fortune, but we'd picked up back pay before we left Brisbane. We had nearly money enough to *buy* a cab.

Nancy led us to a nice house on a short street that ended at a beach. Soon Guppy and I were warmly greeted by a mother and father. Nancy's sister was taking a shower, before going to bed early. Her father produced a bottle of beer and poured. It tasted good, but I felt crummy. I was glad I was going to bed early, too.

Nancy's sister entered the living room, wearing a dressing gown, her dark hair damp.

Tallish. Slender. Dark eyes that flashed a little. Wonderful skin. A slightly upturned nose.

I'd been lovesick over various girls at different times as I grew up. But occasionally I had seen a girl with a special look—a warm light deep in the eyes, a softness in the smile, a delicacy of features, but with an inner strength. It became, to me, *the* special look. Some actresses had bits of it. When I was in college I met two girls with it. One was far too young, a mere teenager. *I* was far too young for the other.

Here it was again, The Special Look.

"This is my other daughter, Jean," said her father. I summoned what voice I could and managed to croak "How do you do." She answered in exactly the same rasp, and we looked at each other, smiling.

So, though neither of us felt up to going out, we somehow did. I don't remember what arguments were falteringly presented and quickly shot down. I do remember that, sick or not, I badly wanted a date with this girl and hoped she would agree. And she did.

I remember a taxi coming to the door. We went to the officers' club. The Mills Brothers' great "Paper Doll" was newly installed in the juke box, and we danced, and it felt fine together.

She asked what I was doing in Melbourne, and I explained that I was waiting for new planes to be properly put together so we could fly them back to New Guinea. I pointed out, perfunctorily, a picture of a Jug on the wall, and she glanced at it without much interest. The whole business of war was as trite and boring to her as to me. She had obviously been pursued by several young men. Many of them, as I later learned, were dead, the most recent burned to a char in a Spitfire.

She talked about her nursing: the rigid discipline of a mysterious martinet known as "Matron," the endless surgical dramas of the "O.R.," the routine of the wards: Men's Medical, Men's Surgical, Women's the same, Ward C, also known as BND for "Bloody Near Dead."

She'd just taken her finals. If she passed (could there be a doubt?), she'd do some sort of war service, of course. Her uncle was in charge of a huge military hospital. Maybe he'd help tee something up for her. We talked endlessly, croaking back and forth with our laryngitis. We barely mentioned tomorrow. We both knew we'd see each other.

For ten days we met whenever she could. I had nothing in the way of it except a routine phone call. One of us ferry pilots made it every morning to the engineering depot. And always the answer was the same: "Sorry, you guys. They're still leaking." And we'd reply, "Hey, no sweat. Make them work right. Be sure."

Then there might be lunch with J, or just a chance to meet during whatever time she could scrape up from her schedule. One lazy autumn afternoon she spent her two hours off-duty by falling asleep under a tree in the Botanical Gardens while I sat beside her and looked at her, and dozed off, too.

With Nancy and Guppy we'd show up at the Embassy, our boots clanking with bottles. We'd dance to "Don't Sit Under the Apple Tree With Anyone Else But Me," and a pretty good imitation of Glenn Miller's "In the Mood," and when the band started on "Paper Doll," J and I would smile and rise from the table.

One night we went to the test pilots' flat and found one of them in a drinking bout with a nightclub waiter. It was a brutal mismatch; not many people can go drink for drink with a test pilot. Pretty soon the waiter went reeling out. Another late-arriving guest said he was lying in the garden, apparently dead.

No one seemed to pay much attention except J, the nurse. She looked at me and said, "Come on," and I went with her down the stairs and out into the cool night.

The man wasn't dead, but he took some rousing. J said we couldn't possibly leave him lying there in the dew. "Perfect way to get pneumonia," she said. So we got him up and I dug out his wallet and found his address, and we set out to get him to his flat a few blocks away.

Humane it may have been. It was also revolting. The man had obviously been very ill as he lay on the ground, and he continued to gasp and heave and choke as we walked him home. I came close to not giving a damn if he lived or died, but J wasn't about to give up on a patient, and we both knew we couldn't just leave him in the gutter.

So we delivered our wretched burden to his displeased landlady and walked back to the test pilots' flat. We took over the bathroom to clean ourselves up. And I looked at this lovely girl who cared about human beings, even a stupid sot she'd never seen before, and I said, "You've got to marry me, you know."

And a few nights later, when she'd learned that she'd passed her finals, we went to do the rides at Luna Park (every Australian city seemed to have a Luna Park) to celebrate. And she said she would.

Looking back today, I wonder what in the world we were thinking of. We had known each other a matter of hours. We had no prospects, no family trust funds, no idea of how we would ever even see each other again, much less marry and live happily ever after. But we both felt empty when apart, and life was exactly right when we were together,

The war intruded only twice. Once was when Guppy and I were in the kitchen of J's house while the girls were fixing a cup of tea. One of them turned on the hot water and the gas heater—the "geyser"—went off automatically: "WHOOSH!"

Instantly, Guppy and I were under the table.

The second time was inevitable. One early morning, the test pilots phoned us squadron pilots at our billet in town, and broke it to us gently that all six P-47s were ready to go, their engines clean and tight, their fuel tanks topped off for a flight to Sydney, first step toward the north. The time had come, as we knew it finally would.

J was home, off-duty until later that morning. I hurried to her house. We had just time to walk to the beach, to talk a little, to hold each other. Then we both had to leave.

"I'll fly over the hospital," I said.

"Don't get too low," she said, "or you'll get into all kinds of trouble."

"I'll be at a thousand feet. I'll blip my engine and waggle my wings."

"That would be fine. I'll get some patients to watch for you and tell me."

At a small airfield beside Melbourne's harbor the new planes were aligned, no olive-drab paint because we were winning the war now, and didn't need camouflage. No squadron colors, either. Just bright silver, dazzling in the autumn sun.

I wrenched my mind from J to the flight. We planned our course for Sydney—northeast until we hit the coast; then follow it northward to the city. We'd hold formation because new planes always had bugs, and we needed to keep an eye on one another.

"I want to break away after takeoff for a few minutes," I told them.

"I'm coming with you," Guppy said, catching on right away. Some of the others wanted to say good-by, too, to people on the ground. We agreed to rendezvous at 5000 feet over an easy landmark on the beach.

"Let me circle the hospital alone," I said to Guppy as we walked to our planes.

"Of course. I'll orbit wide of you."

I climbed up the polished flank of this big, shiny beast, and wormed into the cockpit that, with its bubble canopy, had looked so small from the ground. It was just the same cockpit that I knew so well, but that canopy made me feel I could see forever.

The engine blasted to life, fine and strong, the rpms barely dipping as I checked magnetos. Then I was away, dodging the antennae of a freighter, moored at the end of the strip, thundering up to 1000 feet and heading for the heart of the city. Guppy flew wide on my wing.

I swung the new plane into steep turns, left and right, to get the feel of her, and also get a clear view of the city spread out below me. Prince Henry's Hospital was easy to find with its tall, buff-colored central section. I circled it, shoving the throttle back and forth to produce a roaring and fading of the engine sound.

Four or five turns seemed enough, and I broke away. But this new plane was sweet in the air, the joy of flying was great, and I was young and still reckless. I badly needed to make a proper farewell to this strange, peaceful time, and also get my mind ready for a return to the real world that lay ahead, northward.

I spotted Guppy and we joined up, wing to wing. Then, without a word on the radio, but with full understanding of each other, we lowered our noses and headed for the beachside where I'd said good-by only a few hours before. Guppy glued himself to the rushing sand while I flicked over the rooftops beside him, recognizing streets and crossings. Then, lower still, going like the hammers of hell, I dodged chimneys on a blur of slate roofs. I tried to keep track: Her house must be just about *here*...but it shot past much too fast, like the time.

Easing back on the stick, I laid the nose on a cloud, Guppy beside me, and at 5000 feet we banked around to find the rendezvous. The other four showed up, right on schedule. We took up our course to Sydney and on toward the tropics, to where the islands lay, all professionals again, heading for our job.

Soon after Mueller and I rejoined the Beavers, MacArthur managed to pull off one of the war's greatest and most successful surprises. Hollandia, Japan's biggest New Guinea base, miles beyond Wewak and far nastier, was the last place in the world that any of us thought we'd attack. We hadn't yet made much of a dent in Wewak. But MacArthur suddenly leapt at Hollandia and seized it, fooling everyone, including the Japanese. Grudgingly, we had to admit that the big tin god had really pulled a fast one.

I have a hazy memory of seeing American paratroops boarding transports at that time. The men had painted their faces black and green for camouflage, and they looked proud and tough—the same look that the front-line Australian troops had. It appeared that at last the American infantry had been trained into good shape, and were ready to fight.

But all my memory of this time of warfare is wiped clean by the impact of having a girl I desperately missed and wanted to marry. I took it heavy from the Beavers. Most of them thought I'd gone bonkers and should be shipped home. Steve knew me well enough to realize this was real, not simply combat fatigue.

I wrote my parents, and they were supportive, though reading between the lines, I saw that they, too, thought I was bonkers. I wrote to J, telling her that I would write to ask her father for her "hand"—still the proper thing to do in those days. She answered: "Don't you dare. Let me handle him." Clearly, her family were wholeheartedly opposed to her marrying a Yank. When she broke it to them, they said, "We might have expected this from Nancy, but never from you."

I filled out a form requesting permission to marry an Australian. It warned that this was a very difficult step to take, that the form would have to go through the chain of command right up to MacArthur and back again, that if a superior officer requested it, the army would investigate the girl's Australian family to make sure the helpless, innocent Yank wasn't being taken for a ride by some floozie from the snake pit.

My flying was half-hearted. On takeoff I was too abrupt. I found myself turning steeply right into my wingman before he'd gotten well clear of the ground. So new pilots flying my wing fell behind me as we took off, then swung under me to keep their air speed up. And suddenly I realized that I was doing what Heming had done to me on my early flights, and I was ashamed.

I tried to be very careful, but even during gently weaving escorts toward a target area, I flew raggedly, and was hard to follow. Only when someone called in bandits did I smooth out. Steve, now the C.O., got Doctor Mac to limit my flying. Months before I would have been overjoyed. Now I hated being an exception, feeling useless and prey to growing fears that my long string of luck was running out.

We moved to Biak, an island off the Vogelkop Peninsula— the head of the giant bird that New Guinea somewhat resembles on a map. It was very different from Gusap: coral everywhere: the strip, the ground under our feet, the dust whenever a plane took off. Dust, that is, unless it rained, turning the coral to white paste. And it rained almost on schedule.

I remember the morning shower, always at eight, rolling in from the sea and thundering on our tents. Those of us who had the day off would crouch naked, soap in hand, under the sloping roofs of the tents, to enjoy a warm, clean shower with no taste of chlorine, but only of salt. Salt from the sea, sucked up in the small water spouts we carefully flew around? We thought so, though perhaps it had clung to our tents after blowing in from the tumbling waves.

The timetable storms were one phase of life that was now not just tropical, but equatorial. The heat was powerful, but here muted a little by ocean breezes. They weren't trades here. They were fickle and inconsequential. But we opened our tents wide to them and welcomed them.

We had little to do, day after day, though night after night the enemy bombed us. I flew a few missions. Nothing much. On one day off I joined a friend from the 39th Squadron to explore Biak. He'd studied biology, and so, wearing old sneakers, we poked along the barely submerged coral reef, finding bits of life. We found a bit of death, too. Passing a cave, we glanced in and saw a Japanese helmet. I went in to get it, but left it alone. There was part of a skull inside.

The enemy, according to MacArthur, had been totally routed from Biak, but we kept hearing rifle fire, off in the hills.

And we met "the hunter," a Digger who got up early every morning and lay in wait beside a waterhole, waiting for isolated, starving Japanese soldiers to creep toward it for a drink. Then he'd shoot them, like animals, and strip off anything he could sell or trade to us Americans.

Every evening the hunter would show up. A slender, dark-haired man with strange, distant eyes. He'd barely speak to us. He'd just show a samurai sword or a headcloth of a thousand stitches or a helmet. For a good sword, his price was $60, or one bottle of our whiskey. The hunter made us all uneasy. He was the only Australian any of us had ever met who never smiled.

Steve and I flew a mission to test propellers on the new planes. We flew wing to wing at exactly the same manifold pressure and rpms, to see whether the plane with the "paddle" prop pulled ahead of, or fell behind, the one with the modified paddle. Results were inconsequential, but using the new gimmick, "water injection," was interesting. The water cooled the cylinders, allowing a tremendous surge of power—64 inches of manifold pressure. Our cockpits filled with smoke, and the engines sounded very rough, but the planes shot ahead.

Finally, for all the month of May 1944, I was detached from the squadron to become a tactical instructor at Moresby. My job was to introduce new fighter pilots, all fat and pink and full of military crap, to the realities of air warfare here, to get rid of some preconceived notions and replace them with some sound ones: Fly spread out so you can see—tight formations are good only for the newsreels; always try for a head-on pass—you've got more guns; learn to look *through* the sky, not just at it. That sort of thing.

An old flight form says that I got a lot of time down at the fighter school in Moresby. I remember only a couple of things clearly. One was a mock air battle when my flight of Jugs was bounced by another instructor's flight of P-38s (the two of us had worked it out beforehand), and two of the new pilots got so involved in being aggressive that they brushed wings. The '38 staggered back to the strip and landed safely with the outer three feet of one wing curled back on itself. The Jug lost a little paint on the underside of one wing. It flew again that afternoon.

The other event was getting sick. I was hospitalized with what was called FUO—"fever of unknown origin"—which was common among New Guinea's old-timers, who all had suppressed forms of malaria. I was damn sick for a day or two. All one night I sat upright on my cot, rocking back and forth and shivering. But the new medicines cleaned me up. When I was released, I found orders sending me back to the Beavers, at Biak.

In late June of 1944, I was given a special leave to Melbourne. What happened there is a blur of scenes, flashes of video from a time before that word was commonly used. An endless flight to Sydney, then on south. A taxi through the rain to the Commercial Travelers Club, where my less-than-willing father-in-law-to-be had reserved a room for me. And it was there, in the lobby, buffeted by a swirl of men in raincoats, some leaving, some arriving, that I spotted through the crowd the most incredibly beautiful woman I'd ever seen, and it turned out to be J.

For a moment we became an island in the tidal sea of commercial travelers.

"What's a commercial traveler?" I asked her when we could speak.

"A salesman," she said, and then tugged me toward the door. "We're supposed to be at a buffet lunch in ten minutes."

Or it might have been a morning coffee with someone...a trip to a clothing store...to a jeweler's...a visit with an aunt who had agreed to host a small reception....I know we did all those things, all within three days out of my pitifully small allowance.

We met the rector of Christ Church because J wanted to get married there. She wasn't a churchy person, but that was her wish, and the rector liked her.

He hated me. He'd been a padre in the Australian Army, and he outranked me. He saw me not only as a faithless pagan, but as just another American pilot bent on seducing a lovely and proper Melbourne girl who apparently had refused to give in without benefit of clergy. He made it clear that he considered this a disgraceful situation. "Awkward," he said. "Very awkward. I shall have to call the Bishop."

We sat stiffly in his little Gothic study and looked gloomily at each other, contemplating the prospect of a justice of the peace. But he came back grumbling that the Bishop had approved (God knows why) and that we should come for a rehearsal Monday afternoon at five. "Remember," he said, looking sternly at me, "marriage is not merely for the pleasures of the parties concerned." In other words, it was immoral to get any fun out of sex with your wife. As a New Englander, the offspring of an Early American family with a Puritan background, I wasn't a bit surprised.

That scene remains clear. But others are dim indeed. We got Woody, one of our test pilot friends, to be my best man (Steve couldn't get leave, and Guppy'd been sent home at long last). I had to buy a new tunic because my regular one, seldom unpacked, had vanished forever when a cargo net gave way during our move to Biak. Since the cloth shortage was even more drastic in Australia than in the States, my new tunic was about four inches shorter than regulation, a fact that I got very tired of explaining during the rest of my glorious military career.

Woody prowled through the Melbourne phone book to find some memorably romantic, out-of-the-way honeymoon paradise. Everything was booked solid. He finally got us into the Federal, a funky old hotel near the railroad station. It was notorious as a shack-up joint for Americans and their floozies. We made him and Nancy—J's maid of honor—swear not to tell the family.

Another thing Woody did was persuade me to get pajamas. "I hate pajamas," I told him. "I never wear the damn things."

"You've got to wear them when you're first married," he said. "It's the right thing to do."

"How do you know, Woody? You're not married."

"I just know, that's all. It's always that way in the movies. Always pajamas."

So I got some, dark red with white polka dots. I wore them about five times in all, I guess, then quietly lost them.

Another duty loomed before me: the matter of birth control. With our lives so uncertain, it was essential that we didn't have a baby right away, and I felt it was up to me to handle the problem.

Always, when troops arrived in Sydney on leave, they were issued a few condoms. But Melbourne wasn't a leave town, so I'd have to get them myself. I was sure that you could buy them in a drugstore, but I didn't know what the Australians called them. Condoms? The word wasn't well known, back then, even in the States. Rubbers? I had a feeling that might mean erasers in Melbourne. Prophylactics? I'd probably be given a dozen toothbrushes.

Also, I had to be discreet about this, because in those days you didn't just barge into a pharmacy and announce that you wanted a bunch of French letters, or whatever you called them. You had to find a place that both was empty and had a male clerk, and then you'd sidle over to him and whisper. It took me a while to find a chemist's shop that filled the bill.

The place was old and gray, so shoppers avoided it. And the man behind the counter was equally old and gray—and quite expressionless when he bent to hear me murmur, "I'd like some...um...contraceptives...you know, rubber...or latex, I guess."

"Beg pardon?" he bellowed, cupping an ear.

Just then a woman walked in and started looking at hot water bottles near the door. She moved gradually toward us. It was now or never.

"Contraceptives," I said clearly, turning bright red and sweating inside my shirt.

"Oh, right-oh," the old man bugled cheerfully. "Let's see...condoms...condoms...right here somewhere....Aha! Got 'em! Here you are, captain. Best in Melbourne! Sure that's enough?" And he slapped a rectangular box loudly on the counter. I could feel the woman stare at me with utter distaste, eager to tell her bridge club about this terrible lustful American...an officer, too! So I grabbed the box and reached for my wallet.

"Twelve and six," thundered the chemist. "Condoms have certainly gotten dear in this war. Must pay for your pleasures these days. Thank you, sir, and here's your change. And may I help you, madam?"

And I shot out of there as though the bombs were on their way.

I remember meeting about 2 million friends and relatives. My senses whirled with the parade of attractive girls talking hospital shop with J, of exquisite ladies in the dresses of 1939, when the world of fashion took leave, of tall gentlemen with gray mustaches and limps left over from Gallipoli, of handsome young fellows in uniform who told me I was bloody lucky.

Then the wedding. In no uncertain terms, the rector told Woody and me to stand at attention with our eyes on the altar. And I can't believe, looking back, that the habit of obedience had become so strong that I did so, and never saw my bride come down the aisle.

But suddenly I sensed a soft presence, felt a touch, and turned to look at her, shimmering in white, slender yet strong, eyes flashing a smile behind the misty veil. Everything went fine after that. We were both absolutely sure that we were doing the right thing.

Champagne was almost impossible to get, so all the men tried to get some and we ended up with far too much. We moved a case into the Federal and stowed it under the bed. I borrowed long woollies from my father-in-law to cope with Melbourne's winter weather, which sliced through me like a scalpel. We met more relatives. J felt it was only fair to let them look me over. One aunt, the closest personification of the Victorian era I ever expect to meet, was miffed when we wouldn't reveal where we were honeymooning. "Good heavens," she exclaimed, "the way you two act, anyone would think you were staying at the Federal!"

Yet the old hotel wasn't bad. We discovered that people who are shacking up tend to be quiet about it, and the place was wondrously silent. I don't remember the food, for we always ate breakfast at a little Greek restaurant where we could get steak and eggs, every morning. My bride ate them with such relish that I wondered if I could keep her properly nourished.

We ate other meals out. But in the evenings, after dinner or the Embassy, we'd sit together in our funky room, facing an electric heater, and sipping at that endless champagne.

Then it was over, and I went north again. I got a ride in an A-20, taking the gunner's seat, well aft of the pilot. We started late from Melbourne and the weather socked in, and we landed at a seaside base in New South Wales, where the RAAF flew antisubmarine patrols. The aircrews were bored, and happy to host us, peering into our plane until it was too dark to see, then leading us back to their mess hall for drinks and dinner.

Afterward, they played impromptu rugby in the mess hall, and I made my pilot go to bed because I didn't want him flying with a hangover in the morning. He was sullen about it, but I outranked him.

That was my first small indication that a large chunk of my fighter pilot's innate recklessness had dissipated. Back with the Beavers, I still flew, but with more thought for J and my new life than for my mission. I handled a plane just fine, but now the flights were mostly administrative—a few tests and surveys of the area, for we were soon on the island of Noemfoor and then in Owi, a small quay just off it.

Steve was sent to Group Headquarters, and since I was operations officer, I ran the squadron. Nothing to it in those days, for the missions were routine patrols while all forces geared up for the great push northward, to the Halmaheras, and on to the Philippines. Our Beavers faced extra-long missions using new techniques for saving fuel.

Of course I'd have to fly those missions when they started. I guessed that as acting C.O. I'd have to lead. And that prospect was sobering for a man who for the first time had someone else immediately, deeply involved in his fate.

But as so often happened, the military world in its total blindness solved my problem. On an October morning, right after the eight o'clock rain, I received orders to return to the States.

I'd made it. I'd be "home alive in 'forty-five."

But....

What in the world was going to happen to J? To our marriage? To our future?

Had I been a more important officer, versed in the legalities of the army system, I'd have known how to circumvent my orders—to get sent, perhaps, to Melbourne officially, to spin out a sort of life there, fat-catting away for the rest of the war. But I was only a GI pilot, knowing nothing except to fly my missions and obey orders. I had no friends in high places.

I wondered if I could get leave to Melbourne, a final ten days with J before fate stepped in and separated us. Getting my gear together at the administration tent, I asked my clerk about the leave process. Squadron clerks know everything.

"That's under the C.O.'s authority," he told me. The C.O. was Steve, and he was away on some inspection tour with Group.

"Hey, I'm the acting C.O.," I said. "Can I order myself on leave?"

"Don't see why not," he said. "But the orders will have to be approved by Group, anyway."

"By the group C.O.?" I'd heard he hadn't been overjoyed at my marriage.

"Officially, yes sir. But I know his administrative clerk, and he does most of that kind of work. I'll cut your orders, and give him a ring."

And so, thanks to being good friends with all our NCOs— who really ran the squadron—I was on my way south. I said a hasty good-by to the Beavers, so many of them now new faces, and looked around the briefing tent with its newly issued folding deck chairs, its spruce-new blackboard, it's wood-framed bulletin board with orders and messages affixed with colored tacks. There was even a carefully lettered sign indicating the posted "Dear John" letters.

We were a hot squadron, now. Our gear was new and efficient. The pilots wore tropical flying suits of thin, supposedly flame-resistant cotton, and hacked-off shorts were now frowned on because of antimosquito tactics. No longer forsaken, we Beavers.

So I went south for a final visit. And I recall little of it except that J and I spent a serene ten days at her home. I achieved partial acceptance by her mother and father. At Prince Henry's Hospital, I was introduced to J's fearsome Matron, and J assured me that this dragon lady had never been more charming.

"Married life is a lot of good-bys," J said on one of our last walks along the beach. "Where will you be stationed when you go home?"

"I haven't a clue."

"What are your chances of being sent back here?"

"Not so hot, I'm afraid. But we'll get back together, somehow."

We were accepting, as were thousands of others of our generation, the strange realities of our world—impermanence, personal sacrifice, the constant threat of tragedy, and the brief, rapturous moments of joy. We didn't pause to analyze our lives, back then. And we hadn't been taught the importance of understanding our "identities." We thought we did already. But the strange, often wrenching, and sometimes tragic things that we went through have stayed in our memories, and remain there, still.

Now that we Beavers are well into our seventies, our world of long ago—the good and the bad of it—often returns to us quite clearly for short moments. The sight of a P-47 in a museum brings it all back. So does the sound of a Glenn Miller tune, or the voice of a distant friend on the telephone.

Sometimes I notice the smell of green mold on leather, or the taste of a stale cracker, and these will do the trick. And of course there are always those sudden, strange dreams: dreams of the old Beavers who were taken from us, so long ago.

On the whole, I think it's good to remember.

EPILOGUE

Steve was considered the Beavers' best C.O. He led them through the Philippines campaign and survived it. The Japanese resisted with their Tonys and new Tojos, fast, tough, radial-engine fighters. The squadron shot down many of them, and lost a few to them, and also to the dreadful weather and the normal dangers of those terribly long missions. One loss was Heming, who had persuaded the authorities at the new Pentagon in Washington to send him back to the squadron. There, at last, he fulfilled his death wish. He was one of many others, mostly new lads I barely knew.

Steve, still a good friend, told me years later that one time, after watching the Beavers take off on a routine mission, he started driving his jeep back to the alert tent and suddenly had to stop. Uncontrollable tears were coursing down his cheeks and blinding him. There was no reason for them, just tension.

Even the release from tension could have surprising effects. When I finally got back to the States, I stopped off for a couple of nights with one of my brothers. And walking along a peaceful civilian street near his home in Berkeley, California, I distinguished myself by abruptly wetting my pants. Apparently, that wasn't particularly unusual.

The Beavers that I still see have generally matured successfully. There are a few who are ridden by persistent devils, but most have done well in professions, politics, business, the USAF. They seem an unusually bright group, full of good stories, well told, and thoughtfulness, well expressed. When we see one another's faces and picture them inside a fighter's canopy, long, long ago, our old fraternal closeness returns.

Thank God we're poised enough to handle this surge of affection without mawkishness.

On an early morning in 1992, I drove into Washington, D.C., to greet a new exhibit at the Smithsonian's National Air and Space Museum. It was a P-47 with a bubble canopy, beautifully restored, painted with the colors of a squadron that had served in Europe half a century before.

The plane was introduced at a breakfast reception, and members of the Thunderbolt Pilots Association, Ltd. were gathered to celebrate the display of their darling. I might have introduced myself as a fellow member, but this time I wanted to stay apart. I had memories to sort out.

Staring at the great plane, I tried to recall details of flying it. I came up with a few blurred visions: passing a hand along that smooth wing in the early morning, and feeling heavy dew; clambering up those footholds to the cockpit; the vile smell of the oxygen mask; the agony of being trussed in great discomfort for a long mission; the delight of landing at last, of seeing the airstrip stretching before that big round nose, the slowing, the reaching of those wide-spaced wheels, the chirp and rattle as rubber met the steel matting. We used to undo the straps while still on the landing run, and stand up in the cockpit to feel warm prop wash drying our stale sweat. And we'd rub our numbed buttocks to get the blood flowing again....

The press cameras finally finished with shots of the plane and of its elderly former pilots gathered beside it, and I had a chance to study it closely. It was a D-model, all silver except for its markings and its glittering bubble canopy. I realized it was precisely the same type of P-47 as the one that I flew north from Melbourne half a century before. I remembered my takeoff, when I headed for a ship moored in line with the runway. When I tried to raise my landing gear, after getting off the ground, the little locking lever jammed. I had to use both hands to get the wheels up, and fly with the stick between my knees.

Then I remembered the turns over Prince Henry's Hospital and the way we buzzed the coast to Elwood—a fool thing to do, of course, but not unnatural. That had been a sweet plane, and I gazed now at her sister, there in the museum, as people left to get back to their offices, and the old guys walked away, a little mistily. I guess most of them went on to swap yarns about combat in the D-model. But as I drove home, I couldn't think of any really good stories, even though I too had flown her in combat. The hero stuff had been erased by the rush of my own memories.

Our own memories. When I got home, my wife asked how the reception had gone.

"Fine," I told her. "You'd have enjoyed it. You might have recognized the plane."